out of the blue

Hay House Titles of Related Interest

out of the

blue

True-Life Experiences
of Awakening, Revelation
and Transformation

Mary Terhune

HAY HOUSE

Carlsbad, California • New York City • London • Sydney
Johannesburg • Vancouver • Hong Kong • New Delhi

First published and distributed in the United Kingdom by:
Hay House UK Ltd, Astley House, 33 Notting Hill Gate, London W11 3JQ
Tel: +44 (0)20 3675 2450; Fax: +44 (0)20 3675 2451; www.hayhouse.co.uk

Published and distributed in the United States of America by:
Hay House Inc., PO Box 5100, Carlsbad, CA 92018-5100
Tel: (1) 760 431 7695 or (800) 654 5126
Fax: (1) 760 431 6948 or (800) 650 5115; www.hayhouse.com

Published and distributed in Australia by:
Hay House Australia Ltd, 18/36 Ralph St, Alexandria NSW 2015
Tel: (61) 2 9669 4299; Fax: (61) 2 9669 4144; www.hayhouse.com.au

Published and distributed in the Republic of South Africa by:
Hay House SA (Pty) Ltd, PO Box 990, Witkoppen 2068
info@hayhouse.co.za; www.hayhouse.co.za

Published and distributed in India by:
Hay House Publishers India, Muskaan Complex, Plot No.3, B-2,
Vasant Kunj, New Delhi 110 070
Tel: (91) 11 4176 1620; Fax: (91) 11 4176 1630; www.hayhouse.co.in

Distributed in Canada by:
Raincoast Books, 2440 Viking Way, Richmond, B.C. V6V 1N2
Tel: (1) 604 448 7100; Fax: (1) 604 270 7161; www.raincoast.com

Text © 2015 by Mary Terhune

Cover design: Amy Rose Grigoriou • Interior design: Riann Bender

Permission was given to reprint the following copyrighted material: from *The Subject Tonight Is Love: 60 Wild and Sweet Poems of Hafiz*, copyright 1996 & 2003 by Daniel Ladinsky and used with his permission (pp. 71–72); and *Soul's Journey*, a poem by Aditi Thatte and used with her permission (pp. 109–110).

The moral rights of the author have been asserted.

The information given in this book should not be treated as a substitute for professional medical advice; always consult a medical practitioner. Any use of information in this book is at the reader's discretion and risk. Neither the author nor the publisher can be held responsible for any loss, claim or damage arising out of the use, or misuse, of the suggestions made, the failure to take medical advice or for any material on third party websites.

A catalogue record for this book is available from the British Library.

ISBN: 978-1-78180-705-7

Printed and bound in Great Britain by TJ International Ltd, Padstow, Cornwall.

For my grandson Nicolas.

When Nicolas was one month old,
he came to me in a dream and said:
"God is consciousness,
I am consciousness,
Everything is consciousness,
The people need to know.
I'm glad you're here with me, Mary,
I like the name Mary."

This book is written to fulfill his wish.

contents

foreword

What is the essence of human beings?

Is our essence entirely constituted by the chemical elements and bioelectrical processes that make up our physical bodies? Or is our essence an invisible, spiritual spark or soul that pertains to a nonphysical, higher state of reality?

Mary Terhune is a living example of someone who initially subscribed to the first, physicalist worldview. Yet due to extraordinary, alternate states of consciousness that came upon her unbidden, she woke up to the second, spiritual worldview. This book is her gripping, first-person account of life-transforming experiences of spiritual enlightenment. Mary's work is a fascinating, clearly written spiritual handbook for people who—like herself, and like me—have a restless, unquenchable analytic mind.

In the historical past, mystics and visionaries were regarded as exceedingly rare or even unique individuals who were somehow set apart from the rest of humanity. Visionaries were assumed to have some special, direct point of contact with the divine that was missing among their fellow human beings. Modern research with people who had near-death experiences or spontaneous episodes

of mystical consciousness, however, has shown the direct opposite. Apparently, the propensity to elevated, ecstatic states of awareness—sometimes referred to as "cosmic consciousness"—is an intrinsic property of our human nature. And it seems to me that the implications of that fact are exceedingly profound.

Now, of course, each individual human person is extraordinary, and Mary is no exception. As you will see in reading this book, she has a very inquisitive mind. Mary worked for 16 years at the Massachusetts Institute of Technology, one of the most amazing and respected institutions of higher learning on this planet, as an administrative assistant managing the office and organizing international conferences for the Center for Theoretical Geo/Cosmo Plasma Physics, meeting the top 200 space plasma physicists in the world. Undoubtedly that work environment offered inspiration in her quest to answer the profound questions of human existence: *Who am I? Why am I here? Does death really exist? What is the nature of reality?* Even so, Mary beautifully illustrates my point that people with spontaneous spiritual experiences are like the rest of us. They don't have any special favors conferred on them by God. A mystic who encountered a life-affirming visionary experience could well be sitting in the seat beside you the next time you ride the bus. Or you could well be such a person yourself. Demographic surveys have consistently shown that a huge percentage of people in the normal population have experienced cosmic consciousness of the type Mary describes.

One factor that sets Mary apart among her fellow mystical visionaries is the use to which she puts her otherworldly encounters. Specifically, her life concerns now revolve around one of the most ancient spiritual modalities—healing. In contemporary America, most people unreflectingly subscribe to the canons of scientific, allopathic medicine. And surely the accomplishments of modern medicine are nothing to be sneezed at, for all the millions of lives that have been saved, or at least improved. The success of allopathic medicine tends to make us oblivious to a very important reality: Namely, the very notion of what an illness is, is not a scientific question at all, but rather a philosophical and ultimately perhaps spiritual question. To me, this is the most interesting and significant aspect of Mary's otherworldly visionary journeys. For she has brought back promising insights into the nature of illness and the future directions of the healing enterprise.

I highly recommend Mary Terhune's book on spiritual enlightenment. When you read these pages, you will meet a very reflective, soft-spoken, wise woman who has ventured where someday we too will. I believe you will benefit from her meditations on the meaning of spiritual experiences and their relevance to living a human life on Earth.

— Raymond Moody, M.D., Ph.D.
Author, *Life After Life*

author's note

It was July 2013, midnight, and my cell phone was ringing. Normally I'm in bed by 10 P.M. with my phone shut off for the night, but for some reason, which we will call divine intervention, I was watching an inspiring video and got so caught up I forgot the time. I answered the phone, although I didn't recognize the number of the person calling. "Hello?"

"Is this Mary?" the voice asked.

"Yes, this is Mary."

"Hi, this is Wayne Dyer."

Astonished, I said, "Oh, hi! How are you?"

First, I need to back up to see how we got to this point. About six days prior to the phone call, I was sitting with my co-worker Susie, talking about our lives. I told her, "I just completed a big project and feel like I'm ready to move on to the next thing in my life, the next chapter."

Susie asked, "Well, what would you like to see happen?"

"I'd like my book [which was self-published at the time] to become a bestseller because I believe in its message."

"Then you will have to send it to someone like . . . I don't know . . . hmm . . . Wayne Dyer."

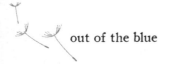

"Really?"

"Yes," she replied. "I think his audience would be interested."

She said this with such conviction that when I finished work, I went home, wrote a note, put it in a copy of my book, and drove to the post office, mailing the package to: *Dr. Wayne Dyer, Best-selling Author, Maui, Hawaii,* with a zip code I thought might work. I didn't know his real address, but I figured this was close enough.

Fast-forward to the late-night phone call—it turns out that Dr. Dyer was very amused by the address label. He said, "You know you've made it when you're sent mail addressed *Best-selling Author* as your street address, and it gets to you!"

Dr. Dyer invited me to come to his Divine Love seminar in Maui the following January, as a surprise guest author. Onstage he read the entire "Self-Realization" chapter of my book, which he said was not only the best description of self-realization he had ever read, but he'd also never read from someone else's book for 20 minutes at one of his seminars!

Tears rolled down my cheeks as I heard Dr. Dyer read my experience of self-realization. His voice was filled with rich tones of deep spiritual longing and understanding, mirroring our yearning for inner freedom—the hallmark of his work. It was well received by everyone.

It was then that Dr. Dyer made the declaration that Hay House was going to publish my book. With a heart full of gratitude to Dr. Dyer and Hay House, my original book has been revised, added to, and edited. Please enjoy this updated version of *Out of the Blue.*

introduction

Humanity now stands at a clear crossroads. We can choose whether to continue living in ego identification, stuck in a story of separation and the suffering it generates, or to awaken to our natural state of divine unified consciousness called *self-realization*. In this state of unified consciousness, we experience living as God with God. We are not "separate co-creators" with God, as some might say, for any separation would imply an ego, but one unified light of omniscience serving our families, friends, and communities, creating heaven on earth.

This book is about my own spiritual journey, from living in the reactive state of ego to living in an awakened state of divine consciousness. I share the challenges I encountered, as well as how I practiced and integrated the spiritual understandings I was given while going about my daily life. Along the way I learned that compassionate love is needed to help each other heal our stories of separation and suffering, allowing us to become fully human as we move toward becoming fully divine.

I was born in 1944 and lived a very ordinary life—that is, until 1984, when miraculously, I had a spiritual

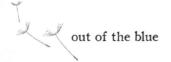

awakening prompted by a visitation from the master Jesus. The Jesus I experienced with this awakening did not espouse any religious dogma or fanaticism. He did not belong to any particular country or religion and yet belonged to all countries and all religions. I believe this is true of all self-realized masters, and I believe this understanding can be true for all of us as well. I was raised Catholic, but at the time of awakening, I wasn't sure I believed in the notion of God and had long ago left the dogma of religion. I had no idea what a spiritual path was or that such a thing even existed. In other words, I was dead asleep in the separative dream of the ego, called my life and story as Mary.

From the moment of awakening with Jesus, and for all the years to follow, my life has been filled with mystical experiences and revelations, including the highest state anyone could experience on this sacred earth: the experience of self-realization. I came to know Jesus as a mystic revolutionary delivering a groundbreaking message that the kingdom of God is within each and every person. At the time of self-realization I was given that same message, that divinity awaits all mankind. I received other messages, too, about how it is humanity's time to rise up and reclaim our divine kingdom through self-realization.

The book culminates in my discovery of homeopathy as a form of consciousness-based medicine, gifted to humanity from Mother Nature, which allows us to heal our physical, emotional, and mental bodies by restoring our consciousness to harmony. Homeopathy is the perfect system of medicine at a time when we are discovering that it is our divine consciousness that infiltrates, innervates, and informs the body. It is in the field of consciousness where our mind and emotions store our traumas, which in turn appear as physical symptoms. Once we experience that we are nothing but consciousness (spirit) innervating and animating a physical body, we will then see the need for a system of consciousness-based medicine to support it and maintain harmony.

As a registered nurse (RN) trained in the allopathic approach to disease, I was amazed when the door to homeopathy opened in my life during a health crisis, offering me an entirely new way and understanding of how to heal. I was equally astonished when I discovered that it was once part of our health-care system—on its way to becoming the most effective, affordable, and curative system of medicine without side effects—before it was systematically removed by competing forces who were claiming it was unscientific!

When you read of the amazing healing stories I share in this book, I hope you'll be inspired to try homeopathy for yourself. Let's reclaim this system of healing once part of, then discarded by, our medical system and reclaim our divine state that has been discarded by ego identity.

I hope that by sharing my story, it will help others know that our lives, including all of our activities and inner struggles, are a sacred path to the divine within. In other words, we do not have to go to a mountaintop; we simply need to go deeply within ourselves. Then we will be led intuitively to the people, places, experiences, and books that will support our inner awakening.

In my case it took a life crisis to awaken to divinity, but that doesn't have to be your case—you can make the choice right now to turn inward and do the work of releasing emotional blocks in order to open to your divine nature. In taking that inner journey to divinity, the answers to the sacred and eternal questions of *Who am I?* and *Why am I here?* are answered. That is what happened to me. It is also helpful to

find the support of others who are on their own spiritual quest to discover the answer to those questions as well.

Divinity is our destiny, and the time to experience this truth has arrived. It all begins with saying yes to one's own divinity to make it a living reality; everything then unfolds rather spontaneously. The path from the suffering of ego-identification to self-realization is the ultimate, divine quest, which begins with answering the call of our spirit (consciousness); followed by tests and trials as we navigate the inner battles between the ego story and our divine nature; ultimately culminating in a full surrender of the suffering ego story, restoring our divine nature and natural bliss as a living reality.

Every person has their own path that unfolds in its own time and in its own way while the destiny is the same: divinity. May my mystic experiences and revelations bring comfort, strength, affirmation, and inspiration to those reading this book as we awaken out of the suffering dream of the ego to self-realization together.

my life story
as mary

I am 71 and the mother of two grown daughters, a grandmother of five, and great-grandmother of two, and I have been single for many years now. I am still practicing in the health field as a therapeutic massage therapist and homeopathic educator in a sleepy New England town.

I grew up in New Jersey, and my younger years were difficult. When I was 11, my mother abruptly deserted my father, leaving him to raise my brother and me (two older siblings had already left the household). I was the youngest and felt the brunt of that abandonment, as I was very attached to my mother and wouldn't see her again until age 15; by then, the damage had been done and an emotional wall of silent pain built. This was the 1950s, and divorce was a shocking event at that time.

It was also a time when it was thought best not to talk about anything upsetting—just pretend nothing had happened, and go on with your life. The result was that even though I was just 11 and clearly in need of a mother, no

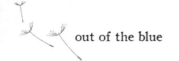

one in my family ever asked how I was feeling or coping. Instead, I was expected to go on with life and take over the role of mothering myself and performing household chores. My child's mind and heart interpreted this as "your feelings don't matter, your needs don't matter, *you* don't matter."

From the time I was very young, I always had an interest in medicine and healing. I began my career in health directly out of high school, after receiving a scholarship to attend nursing school in 1962. But just as I was about to begin my third and final year of nursing school, I became pregnant after a brief encounter with a man I had just met; it was my first sexual experience. I was haunted by the guilt and shame reserved for girls who had sex outside marriage. I was also forced to give up my baby for adoption, being told that I would ruin her life if I didn't; this was the mind-set of the culture at that time.

The traumatic loss of my baby would cast a cloud of regret over the rest of my life. And the core trauma of the broken mother/child relationship of both my mother and my baby would take a lifetime to resolve and have a negative impact on building healthy relationships.

Despite all of this, I was able to complete nursing school in 1966. With diploma in hand, I began my career as an RN working in hospitals, a doctor's office, and nursing homes. I married in 1969, gave birth to a daughter in 1971, and moved from New Jersey to a nice home in western Massachusetts. From the very beginning, though, my marriage was doomed as I didn't really love my husband. It was more of a friendship, but I felt that perhaps it could turn into a genuine love connection.

After moving to Massachusetts, I decided to further my education and obtain a college degree. I was a little rusty in math skills, so I enrolled in some introductory classes at a local community college. I had a powerful inner drive to grow and learn, but this wasn't shared in my marriage. When things didn't go well with my husband, I suggested that we both have counseling; when he refused, I knew I could not stay. After struggling in this relationship, I finally obtained a divorce in 1973. I was now a single mother with full custody of my daughter, Deborah.

Despite my strong desire to grow and learn, I had absolutely no awareness of any inner spiritual life; I was living in the dream of the ego with a debilitating lack of self-esteem and worth. This was aided by the numbing effects of tranquilizers I had been taking since my early 20s, when a doctor suggested it would help me with the anxiety that had begun after I relinquished my baby for adoption.

In the midst of my crumbling marriage, I had met a woman who was also getting a divorce and had children of her own. We became friends based on mutual struggles and a shared interest to move to Boston for college and employment. This friendship developed into a physical relationship as well, and I realize now that the emotional support and nurturing I received was most attractive to me, having had none of that growing up. Without really understanding it, I looked to get from that relationship what I did not receive from my mother, like putting a Band-Aid on a wound.

I would repeat this briefly in other relationships, until I could finally begin to heal the emotional pain of my mother's abandonment and the trauma of giving away my baby. It would be a long and messy struggle to heal these wounds, but in the end I could stand as a more emotionally strong person, more aware of not looking to get from others what I needed to find in myself.

I would also come to know that all the pain of my life, for whatever reason, had to happen the way it did in order for my soul to ripen. It was out of suffering that I would

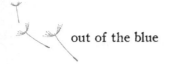

develop a deep compassion for myself and others; it was out of suffering that I came to see that all people suffer, all people carry guilt and shame. It was also out of suffering that my mind finally stopped in a paralyzing state of despair, and the divine swooped in to reclaim itself. First, though, I had to live through a number of life's sorrows, challenges, and difficulties.

I did move to Boston in my new relationship. We eventually purchased a two-family home and rented the first floor out to mutual friends, a husband and wife, with a semicommunal way of living in mind. Even though I started feeling unsettled in my relationship, it was easier to suppress those feelings than deal with them, focusing instead on finishing college. I received a degree in sociology, graduating with honors.

I went on to find short-term jobs at Radcliffe College and Harvard's School of Public Health, providing support for staff. Thanks to those work experiences and my nursing background in hospitals, I was hired as an administrative assistant to the director of a new research administration department at a Boston-based hospital, where I worked until 1985. It was during those early years at the hospital that my whole life turned upside down, as I fully admitted to myself that I was extremely unhappy and needed to change everything about my life. This included leaving the relationship I was in, selling our house, and moving out.

My anxiety was absolutely crippling by now, even as I continued to rely heavily on tranquilizers. The continuing arguments in my relationship—along with the other couple, who did not want me to sell the house—drew more intense as my desire to change and grow as a person

became paramount. I began psychotherapy to deal with the discord and to unravel the mystery of my own emotions.

I also decided to try a series of massage therapy treatments to ease my anxiety, and the results were so wonderful that I entered the field of alternative medicine by enrolling in a part-time, three-year massage therapy school. Once I walked through those doors, I left the allopathic world of drugging myself with tranquilizers behind, and began the long journey of restoring my emotional health through this form of bodywork (along with psychotherapy). Still, all I had learned in Western medicine served as a solid foundation, which I incorporated into my new studies in natural healing.

Psychotherapy gave me the support I needed to develop the emotional courage to leave my situation. I started the long journey of revisiting feelings over the loss of my mother and baby, feelings that were frozen in time inside my heart and mind. None of this was easy, because as soon as I stopped masking those feelings with tranquilizers, they came to the surface with great force, in an ocean of tears. I couldn't hold it back anymore, even if I wanted to. Having announced my intention to leave, I began living in my own separate space in the house, which gave me the chance to feel my own feelings and think my own thoughts. In truth I was still a very emotionally dependent person, but some force propelled me forward to get out of this mess and turmoil.

As I slowly decreased my dependence on tranquilizers and allowed feelings to flow, I started to experience what I can only say were moments of bliss, even in the midst of chaos. These moments would take hold of my being as I danced around for hours by myself in my room. I had no context for this bliss at the time, as I knew nothing about spirituality or of *kundalini,* the sacred energy that flows

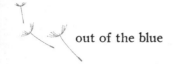

through the body. All I knew was that those moments of bliss gave relief to my emotional suffering, and even though I questioned the concept of God, I felt as if this God I didn't believe in was calling after me.

Near the end of 1982, I had just begun my second year at the massage school, and I met a man to whom I was deeply attracted. I would have happily jumped out of the situation I was in and into his arms if he had reciprocated my feelings, but that was not the case. Still, in his presence I felt a remarkable sense of wholeness and a deep yin and yang harmony I had never experienced before. In retrospect I can see that if I'd fallen into that relationship, it might have kept me from a spiritual awakening, as I would have stopped striving to dive deeply into my interior life. I was looking for a comfortable, easy existence—if I'd have found it, I would've cruised along in it and not questioned life any more deeply. I simply would have made this man the hero of my life instead of reclaiming myself, which was proving to be extremely painful. I would have happily had him fulfill my childhood dream of a white picket fence and perfect family, something I never did experience.

It got to the point that no one in the house was speaking to me, as I was the one who was changing and they wanted things to stay the same. Being on the receiving end of a nasty silent treatment that went on for months and feeling the pressure to leave, I signed a contract selling my portion of the house for a mere pittance of what it was worth, without hiring my own lawyer or agent to protect my interests. It was a financial disaster. What was I thinking at the time, you might ask. The truth is, I had no sense of worth.

The day came when finally, in the spring of 1984, Deborah and I moved into the downstairs of a two-family home owned by an elderly couple. Now, realizing the magnitude of my financial mistake and reeling from the emotional turmoil involved in moving, I found myself sobbing uncontrollably in my living room. Little did I know in the midst of that crisis that I would experience an astonishing spiritual awakening—one that would set me on the path of return to unity with the divine self.

CHAPTER 2

awakening: jesus speaks

It was a Saturday in May 1984, and my daughter was away visiting her father. I was sitting on the couch in my living room, consumed by fear and anxiety, berating myself. This day was the culmination of a lifetime of negative feelings: abandonment, unworthiness, shame, guilt, humiliation, and self-reproach. A feeling of deep despair came over me as I wondered how I would survive emotionally and financially. I felt like a complete loser—through my own fault, I had lost my life savings in the house—and was at my lowest point. The difficulty of life overwhelmed me, and I felt I could not escape it.

My mind searched for answers, but could find none. I felt weighed down by all my thoughts. How could I have been so stupid as to allow myself to lose my investment in the house? Now I was in deep debt with nowhere to turn. I had been so affected by these events that I was on the brink of losing my job at the hospital. I was unable to shake a feeling of doom.

At some point my mind could no longer think . . . I just surrendered everything to my misery.

Having reached the end of all hope, finding myself on the brink of emotional collapse, I put my head in my hands and began to sob uncontrollably, deeper than I ever thought possible. I felt my own shortcomings, as well as all the losses and disappointments throughout my life. In essence, my existence felt like one long burdensome event after another. Why did happiness seem so elusive? Would this be the way I would go throughout life? Was that all there was for me? Had this been preordained? I once heard someone say that when you cry, you don't cry for just one thing, you cry for everything. And this everything I called my life was filled with overwhelming sadness, my own failures, and confusion.

My sobs turned into wailing from the depths of my soul, as the story of my life played out like a movie on the screen of my mind. I saw myself as a young child, so delighted with nature and animals; then my family fell apart after my mother left, and I felt the devastation of it more deeply than ever. Then I saw myself as a young teen, lost and angry, and at the age of 19, pregnant with a child I was forced to give up for adoption. The picture moved to my marriage in my late 20s, which resulted in the birth of my younger daughter but ended in divorce. I saw myself seeking refuge in relationships, trying to get from them what I felt I lacked. This left me feeling helpless and incomplete. The picture fast-forwarded to my present circumstance, in which I had lost all the money I had worked so hard for over the years. I felt all was lost and could not be fixed. I felt my life was lying at my feet in total ruin. I sobbed until I thought I would die.

The pain became so unbearable that I found myself calling out to a God I had long felt deserted me, to a God

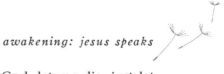

I was sure did not exist: "Please, God, let me die, just let me die. It's too painful, it's too hard." I felt myself falling off a cliff into an endless pitch-black abyss. I tumbled farther and farther, feeling that there was no bottom to it, and wondered where I was going. I let myself fall. I simply didn't care anymore. I thought about how I had lost everything. *How could I let this happen?*

As I asked the question, all of a sudden I started to view my life and myself from the perspective of a compassionate witness. I heard this witness voice say, "This child, teen, and adult you condemn could not help these things. She always had a loving heart; she did the best she could given the circumstances. You can't condemn her. She didn't know." These words entered me very deeply, and I felt the kind, benevolent energy of them. I felt a wave of self-forgiveness wash over me. I had no idea where it came from.

As I started to forgive myself, simultaneously and automatically, I felt my heart release its emotional knots. I had never really understood how to forgive myself before, but now I was somehow being given the experience of it. The depth of this self-forgiveness was deeper than I ever thought possible. It was as if there was no one to forgive but myself. What a curious and liberating feeling.

I felt so free and light in my body, almost as if I could fly. I then saw pictures in my mind's eye of everyone I felt had ever let me down. I saw that they too had only done the best they could. They too had lived their lives mostly out of the need to survive and to make it in this world. Like me, their actions were driven by fear and from the sense of not having enough.

As this feeling of deep forgiveness began to enter my heart, a miraculous event occurred. A great wave of light poured in through the front windows of my living room and began to fill the entire room. My sobs now quiet, I

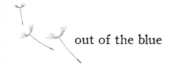

watched in awe from where I was sitting on the couch. Everything felt as if it were moving in slow motion: my mind, my thoughts, and my body. The light was a soft, golden yellow color—it was as if the sun itself had entered the room, washing over everything and covering me like a blanket. I felt incredibly peaceful. This force was so strong that I could not sit up anymore and had to lie down. I felt a deep, loving presence come over me, soothing every cell in my body, and I could not keep my eyes open in its force.

In my mind's eye, I saw a manger and the little baby Jesus appear in my heart region. *What's this?* I thought. The familiar Christmas story played out in my mind, with the Virgin Mary being refused a room in the inn and the Jesus child having to be born in a manger. I had a thought, or perhaps I heard it: *Are you not like him?* The words echoed in my mind: *Are you not like him? Are you not like him?*

The strains of an old familiar gospel song, "Sweet Little Jesus Child," filled my mind. I somehow had an immediate understanding from this song that we, each of us, were this little holy child, and this holy child represented our goodness. It was an innate goodness that we had all but forgotten. I saw how forgetfulness of our true nature kept us acting out of fear—fear of not having enough, fear of not being enough—and I saw how we justified our actions based on this fear.

Then those familiar words from Jesus came to me: "It is easier for a camel to go through the eye of a needle, than for a rich man to enter into the kingdom of God" (Mark 10:25).

These are words I would come to understand more deeply in the years to come, but at that moment I can only say that I found them very comforting.

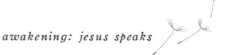

As I lay on the couch absorbing the golden light, I reveled in it. I felt as if all of my burdens were being lifted, and a calmness came over me that was unlike anything I had ever experienced. I became very still, and my breathing slowed down. I felt calm and protected, with all the energy centers of my body flowing freely. Then I noticed something strange about my breathing: instead of breathing from my lungs, I seemed to be breathing from a space that ran adjacent to my spinal column, deep inside me. I remembered hearing about yogis who could somehow breathe when buried alive. I wondered if this was the deep inner breathing center they were able to access, enabling them to stay alive.

As I lay there feeling peaceful and quiet, I heard a distinct voice speak to me, unlike any other I have ever heard. Immediately, I knew who it was. It was the master Jesus.

The First Revelation: On Forgiveness

I could hardly believe it was him! His voice felt at once so familiar and unique. It seemed to hold a feeling in it that I could only equate with the softest, most compassionate love I had ever experienced. Jesus said, "Now do you understand what true forgiveness is?"

As he spoke these words, I was infused with his divine light, which contained the full knowledge and wisdom of forgiveness. In familiar computer terms, the information and experience of forgiveness were somehow "downloaded" into my being, into all my cells, infusing them with the wisdom and knowledge inherent in his words. It was an instantaneous transfer of information on all levels of my being in a flash of light, so to speak.

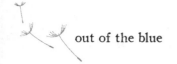

out of the blue

When Jesus posed the question on forgiveness, the example of my own life stood before me as if on a movie screen. As I reframed myself as a compassionate witness of my life instead of a critical judge, I saw and felt my entire being become the embodiment of forgiveness. Blame fled from me in the face of this divine understanding, and I neither blamed myself nor others. I understood that things had to happen in my life the way they happened; there was nothing to change and no one to blame. I felt pure love inside; I felt free.

I understood that forgiveness was really self-forgiveness—that was the crux of his teaching, and I saw how it applied to my life. Since I could not control the events, how could I blame myself? Rather, I needed to find compassion for myself and accept what happened. I wouldn't condone it, but accept with a nonjudgmental state of mind, saying, "Yes, this happened and this is how I felt." If I didn't, then I would continue to relive the experience over and over in my mind, trapped by the thought, *Why did this happen to me? That should not have happened to me.* I would continue to suffer, with no release from the hurt.

Jesus made the experience of self-forgiveness very clear, calling it "true forgiveness." I had always thought that forgiveness was something I did for other people. In truth, true forgiveness would start with myself, by accepting what had happened and having compassion because I could not change it.

It would never be about forgiving the offender—there would be no need to concern myself with that, for when an issue was resolved in myself, as far as I was concerned, it would no longer exist in thought. The other person involved in an event would need to do their own processing, although if it felt right to me I could say I forgave them.

The result of true forgiveness is that I would be emotionally free, not identifying with the hurt anymore.

On this day, beyond any shadow of a doubt, I knew forgiveness as something I did for myself. I had always tried to understand forgiveness on an intellectual level, but Jesus gave me the experience of it. I was so grateful for this, as I felt freed from the suffering of having to be burdened by angry thoughts about anyone who treated me badly. Now I knew I didn't have to hold on to bad feelings. True forgiveness took courage—could I be that courageous?

When I understood and experienced all that Jesus had to say on forgiveness, he moved on to another subject.

The Second Revelation: On Judgment

Jesus spoke again: "Judge not, lest ye be judged." As I heard those words, the experience, wisdom, and knowledge contained within them infused into my being in the same way as the teaching on forgiveness. Immediately, I had the inner experience and understanding that "Judge not, lest ye be judged" literally meant that to judge another was to judge myself right then and there! I had always thought that the phrase meant that you shouldn't judge someone for fear *they* will judge *you* at some future date. But this was not true.

With this phrase, I had an understanding that seeing something negative in someone else was more a reflection of what I didn't like in myself, so if I judged someone, it would instantly come back to me in an injurious way like a boomerang. Life was meant not for judging each other, but for helping each other through. The statement on judgment tied in very beautifully to Jesus's teaching on forgiveness. If I forgave and didn't judge myself, then

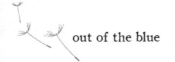

automatically I would forgive and not judge others. It seemed too simple and so obvious. I realized that the truth *is* simple but *not* so obvious.

I was also taken aback by what Jesus was saying about judgment, as I sifted through the files of my mind to count how many times I had judged another. I looked at what judging was, and saw it as a critical approach when viewing another. Why did I do it? Did I need to feel right because I felt so wrong? Clearly I had a lot of inner work to do to release this automatic mental habit. Why didn't I just see the best in another person instead of their weaknesses?

I realized that this mental habit very definitely started with how I viewed myself. If I was self-critical and condemned my own weaknesses, then this habit of negative thinking spilled out onto the world I viewed every day. I knew it would take a concerted effort on my part to turn the bad habit into a good one. I needed to develop the habit of seeing the strengths in others, but knew it meant starting to see the strengths in myself. It had to start with self-forgiveness and not judging myself.

When Jesus finished giving me the experience and knowledge of judgment, he moved on to the next topic.

The Third Revelation: On the Bible

When Jesus said, "Now do you see how they misuse my words in the Bible?" I simultaneously was given the physical, emotional, and intellectual understanding of this question. What he said was actually a statement and question all rolled into one, and it had many meanings. I was infused with his inner thoughts: *Now do you see how people misuse my words against each other to validate their hatred and judgment? Now do you see how they take my words*

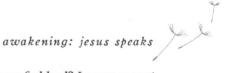

and use them as weapons to make others feel bad? I never meant for that to happen.

As I heard these thoughts, I also felt Jesus's compassionate love. He understood the human egoic struggle; it is always easier to hate than to love. It is always easier to blame because most people live in the ego mind, which is bound by the notion that it's "me against you."

I recognized "they misuse my words in the Bible" also meant that sometimes Jesus was not always understood and, therefore, not quoted correctly. Sometimes the truth in his words had been lost or misinterpreted, and I felt his profound sadness that this had happened. I knew that he never wanted to become a weapon to be used by religions to make people fear him or God. He never wanted to become the property of a particular religion.

I understood that Jesus's words stood on their own. They were not to be held hostage by any particular caste, sect, religion, idea, theory, dogma, nation, country, or people. The truth of his words needed to be experienced and understood inside, in the heart, and never used in judgment against another. Some might wonder how we can know what Jesus really said and what he really meant. My only answer is the knowing will not come from the mind or someone's research; it will come from a knowing in the heart left for each of us to discover, revealed in the experience of our divine nature.

As I wondered how humanity had gotten so sidetracked from Jesus's original meanings, he spoke again.

The Fourth Revelation: On Weight and Emotions

Jesus said to me, "Now do you see what weight problems are all about?" As he spoke the words, he also gave me

the experience and knowledge of the origins surrounding emotions and extra pounds. He infused my being with this knowledge, and I immediately felt my thoughts and feelings as energies.

I saw these energies swirling around my physical body, feeding into it. I started examining my feelings of self-hatred, anger, and sadness as energies; they had a certain heaviness to them that hung in my consciousness, blocking the natural flow of light and love within my being. My body then reflected what I was thinking and feeling: These feelings and thoughts were heavy suitcases of accumulated sorrow and disappointment that I carried around. I saw how the weight of my emotions manifested as physical weight in order to bring my attention to unattended feelings and issues.

My own life experience flashed before me. When I began to receive massage treatments, I got in touch with and released long-held hurt feelings, and that is when I started to lose weight. Releasing the pent-up sadness and grief made me feel lighter inside, and this was reflected in my physical body.

As I was given the experience and knowledge of these issues surrounding weight, I felt my energy centers, the chakras, open from the top of my head down to the bottom of my spine. I felt them mainly in the front of my body as energy points opening and whirling around. I understood that the more I released negative thoughts in my mind and emotions, the more freely these energy centers would spin. I experienced that the chakras were composed of divine light and were an extension of the light of my soul infusing my body.

I remembered reading that the main seven chakras were located along the spinal column, starting at the top of the head going down to the end of the spine, and that each chakra had an endocrine gland associated with it. I knew the endocrine glands were responsible for the psychological and physiological health of the body. As I felt these chakras open and spin on the surface of my body, I became increasingly more peaceful and felt a sense of wholeness. I understood that tightly held emotions and negative thoughts impeded flow in the chakras, and therefore impeded the endocrine glands from functioning at their optimal level. Everything that began in my thoughts (mind/consciousness) ended up being expressed in my physical body, which included weight. It seemed to me that the more I could release on a mental/emotional level, the healthier I would be on a physical level.

It was incredible to feel the light energy of my soul consciousness moving freely in my body, and I had the direct experience of being able to somehow absorb this light as nourishment. It was a strange experience. I felt myself breathing this light into every cell of my body, and I felt so completely full and satisfied on every level. Later in my spiritual journey, I would read a verse from the Bible that spoke to this experience of eating this light filled with divine knowledge: "It is written, Man shall not live by bread alone, but by every word that proceedeth out of the mouth of God" (Matthew 4:4).

For weeks after my experience with Jesus, I needed very little food. What I did eat was rice and vegetables and a little chicken, very simple and pure, which I cooked myself. I never felt very hungry. In fact, I felt as if I fed off the light as sustenance, as nectar. The more I seemed to live in the light, the more satisfied I felt on every level. I wondered if it could be this way all the time. In the days and weeks that followed, my body weight dropped from 119 to 100 pounds. At five feet three inches, I was quite slim, and felt healthy and very energetic.

I wondered why, of all the things that Jesus could talk to me about, he chose weight and emotions as it related to the energy system of the body. I could only assume it was because I chose to be in the healing profession and would need to understand this, not only for myself, but also to share with others.

When Jesus finished imparting his knowledge about weight, emotions, and the chakras, he moved on to the next subject.

The Fifth Revelation: On Disease

Jesus said, "Now do you understand what disease is all about?" As he spoke these words, Jesus gave me the understanding that all disease in our physical bodies begins first on an energetic level as thoughts and feelings. These thoughts and feelings are stored in our mind, and the mind is made of consciousness that surrounds and gives life to our physical bodies. The mind is not generated from the physical body but rather exists outside of and informs the physical body.

Once again, I felt the experience of this knowledge inside my own being as he downloaded his understanding into me. I had a vision of thoughts and feelings hovering around my physical body, feeding their energy into it. And again, I saw the experiences of my own life. Hadn't my migraines been cured as I faced the anger built up from the hurt and sorrow in my childhood? Telling the truth of my life had begun to quite literally set me free. Hadn't my lower-back problems all started with deeply held anxieties that so wracked my body it caused discs to herniate? Hadn't my panic attacks been caused by my inability to address and express my deepest emotional wounds? I knew all this was true.

The medical community has long noted that depression can run in families, and stress can affect your susceptibility, activating the trait or making it worse. Stress is a by-product of mind/emotions, which we all know affects our psychological and physical health—the mind/body connection. The question, then, is how do we keep our consciousness flowing in a state of balance?

I saw how I could affect my health in a positive way, by addressing unresolved mental/emotional issues on the thought/feeling level before they manifested on the physical level in order to get my attention.

In the West, we've been taught a mechanistic view of health, focusing mainly on the physical body as a machine of complex hormones and chemicals and using drugs to manipulate those complexities. But the starting point for physical health is understanding the disharmony of thoughts and emotions on the level of consciousness, the energy of which flows around and innervates the body.

I saw that guilt should not play a role when we look at our health—we must be completely compassionate with ourselves. Sometimes we're just destined to experience disease as a teacher when we cannot learn a life lesson any other way.

As I lay on the couch, all these thoughts and understandings flowed through my mind, one after another. I realized if we had better access to various healing modalities that cure on the level of consciousness earlier in our lives, perhaps we would develop less physical and mental pathology later.

I marveled at all Jesus had imparted to me about disease. The knowledge felt so familiar—had I once known this and somehow forgotten it? All he said had a feeling

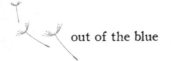

of innate truth to it and would serve as a foundation for future growth and greater understandings as I matured spiritually. Disease had always fascinated me, from the time I was a young child. For me, the study of disease had become a doorway into the study of the infinite.

Once I understood what I needed to know on disease, Jesus moved to another topic.

The Sixth Revelation: On Aging

Jesus said, "Now do you understand what aging is all about?" As he spoke these words, I was given the experience and understanding of aging. I understood that it is caused by the friction between my mind and body, as my mind latched on to thoughts of anger, doubts, fears, and anxieties. As my mind busied itself with one concern or another, I felt how aging was affecting my physical body through the mind/body connection.

I saw how my emotions constantly took me on a roller-coaster ride up and down. My mind was always thinking so many things at the same time, even conflicting thoughts of love and hate. Always regretful of the past or worried about the future, I had no idea how to be in the moment to let my whole being rest. Mental stress has been shown to have a negative effect on our biological systems, taking years off our lives—this, I realized, was the human condition.

The mind is always traveling from one thing to another to try to find happiness. It goes from one thought to another, one activity to another, at a frenetic pace, just to have a moment of satisfaction. In the end, it only feels exhausted, disappointed, and unfulfilled. I understood how negative thinking about others and ourselves creates neurobiological reactions that negatively impact our immune system and speed up the aging process. Chronic sorrow and grief have been shown to affect our hearts and our neurological systems as well.

If I stored negativity in my mind—which is a part of the consciousness that surrounds and feeds into my physical body through its energy centers, the chakras—it would interfere with the harmonious flow of the life-giving force of consciousness. Perhaps if I could quiet my mind, releasing anxieties, and live more in the moment of pure being with its rejuvenating power of peace, contentment, and equanimity, it would slow down the aging process.

I realized that I accepted falling apart as I aged to be inevitable. But I wondered, _Is it inevitable?_ Of course the body would eventually wear out, but perhaps not as quickly and to such a degree as I had previously thought if our minds were more at peace.

I knew I needed to find a better way to handle the anxieties and thoughts that seemed to have free rein in my mind, so they wouldn't continually turn around and around spewing negativities, wearing me out mentally and physically.

I remembered someone telling me that whenever I felt anxious, I should just start taking long, deep, slow breaths, as that would slow down the anxious thoughts. They said that breath regulates the life force, the consciousness of the body and the mind. Therefore, if I consciously slowed my breath, the mind would also slow down and the anxiety would diminish. Controlling the breathing pattern controls the mind, which maximizes the energy and vitality of the body because of the unhampered flow of the life force. I wondered if that was why tortoises lived so long, because they only breathe four times a minute.

When Jesus finished imparting knowledge about aging, he moved on to the final topic.

The Seventh Revelation: On the Ego

Instead of Jesus making a statement about the ego, he went directly into *impressing* me with his thoughts regarding it, giving me an immediate inner experience and understanding. I saw there was this thing called ego: I was given to understand it as an energetic mental construct, a state of mind, so to speak, that we use to create an individual identity and story separate from God, which is our true and natural state of conscious awareness and being. When we identify ourselves as a separate persona from our divine nature, we take on an identity as an individual with a life story and begin to live a story of separation and suffering, with associated likes and dislikes. There is usually one theme of wounding in our life, and we identify with that story. It keeps us stuck in our identity as an individual rather than as a divine being whose nature is bliss.

Upon identifying ourselves as an individual, we construct concepts and ideas about the world and what is good and what is bad. We defend what we like and oppose what we don't like, all of which we feel a need to express. We feel a need to voice these opinions because in identifying with the ego as ourselves, we feel our opinions *are* who we are. All of this we do unconsciously. We then feel offended if someone doesn't agree with our opinions. Hence there is no end to our suffering!

I became aware for the first time that the ego was just a state of mind, stuck in the belief that my true nature is living as a separate individual rather than as a unified divine being. I realized that we *have* an ego but are *not* an

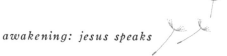

ego. The ego felt like a tool of the mind that I used in order to navigate my way around the world and deal with people. I experienced it as a reactive tool ready to defend against any real or imagined insult or position contrary to my own ideas.

In a nutshell, the ego is a state of mind that feels separate from God; its function is to maintain its life by keeping us stuck in our stories, identifying and reacting to these stories to keep them going. Without the ego, there would be no story to identify with, and we would then melt into our true divine nature as God, moving from a dualistic state of mind into a state of conscious oneness.

Understanding the ego in this way was truly enlightening. Without being conscious of it before, I saw how I used the ego as a way of identifying myself as a woman, a mother, a nurse, a massage therapist, and so on. I identified myself as the different roles I played in life, and then either congratulated myself for doing a great job or, more often than not, condemned myself for not measuring up. As I lay on the couch that day, I found myself asking questions: *If I am not the ego, then who is this real me? Is it the role I'm playing at the moment? Could I actually get free of the ego somehow, or do I always have to have one?*

I remember being taught from those in the field of psychology that you needed to have an ego or you wouldn't be able to function in the world. Now I questioned if that was true. *Will I always be subject to its whims and fancies, constantly defending its positions and opinions? But how can it be so important to defend my positions and opinions when those change over time? How important can they be? So if I'm not my opinions and ideas and I am not my ego, then who am I? My roles? No, those change, too.*

As I contemplated these questions, the faces of different people I had known appeared in my mind, like on a

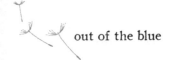

movie screen. As each person appeared, somehow I could see how they used their egos to define themselves and defend against their unresolved hurts. I was able to see how their unresolved emotional and mental traumas acted out: I saw how some were hiding their hurt behind anger because the original pain was unspoken and unresolved. The hurt and anger would then come out sideways in the way they interacted in the world. Some were blatantly disagreeable and hard to get along with. Some were overly sweet, while rage boiled beneath the surface. Some were controlling. Some used others for their own purposes in very underhanded ways. Some were filled with pride, overcompensating for their lack of self-esteem. I saw this was the state of humanity, including myself.

I saw how I had behaved in these different ways at one time or another in my life, and I began to sob for my own human predicament and out of remorse for my past behavior. I understood that we humans suffer a great deal protecting our egos. We spend a lot of time trying to get the upper hand, jockeying for positions at the expense of others, arguing and simply making others feel bad while we felt all the better for it. The ego is such a destructive force that just to put a crack in it to begin to open to the light often takes a big crisis in a person's life.

I saw how I lived my life completely dead asleep to anything but the ego's stories. I acted according to its rules, and I was horrified. I thought of Jesus's words, "Forgive them; for they know not what they do." I understood the ego is such a tenacious force that some kind of experience of our divine nature is needed to know we have a choice to live in our divine nature or the ego nature; this is what free will is all about. It seemed the only purpose of the ego is to hold us in a self-critical suffering mode to keep us separate from our divine nature.

This experience and understanding of the ego was the beginning of a true spiritual awakening within me. As I lay on the couch, aware of these thoughts and impressions, I again felt the presence of an inner love that seemed to be at the core of my being. My hard emotional edges were melting away, and I felt serene and gentle. Was love the true essence of everything and everyone? It seemed so, but it was so covered over by the antics of the ego.

Now that I had become aware of the predicament I faced with regard to the ego, it dawned on me that I had walked through a portal of understanding into a new awareness, and I could never go back to not knowing. I could not justify bad behavior in myself anymore. I felt a deeper compassion for myself and everyone in understanding the stronghold the ego has over all of us.

As I lay on the couch, I felt so much light and love pouring in, around, and out of me. I felt totally peaceful and in awe of all that was happening. The deep, overwhelming despair I felt earlier had completely left. I felt so relieved. I knew that everything was going to be all right. Then, the presence called Jesus left the room just the way he'd entered. As he withdrew his rays through the window, my awareness seemed to return to a normal state of consciousness.

Slowly, I got up and stumbled off the couch, feeling completely transformed. I felt like a different person with a different outlook and different understanding of life. Every cell in my body seemed to pulsate with love. I felt so expanded and serene. By now, it was late afternoon, and I decided to get some fresh air. My legs felt wobbly as I went through the dining room and kitchen, and headed toward the back door to go outside.

out of the blue

Nothing could have prepared me for what I was about to see as my hand reached for the doorknob and pulled the door open.

CHAPTER 3

a veil removed

When I stepped out on the back porch, I could hardly believe my eyes. As I looked out at the lawn, I could see a new dimension: Everywhere I looked was filled with sparkling white light particles, like a Christmas tree with tiny bulbs. Each blade of grass was seemingly made of these shimmering particles; I could still see the green blades, but light twinkled from each one of them!

The backyard had a beautiful apple tree in the middle of the lawn, and flowerbeds and bushes around the perimeter. I looked at the tree, and it sparkled as well, in just the same way as the grass did. The flowers and bushes, a scampering squirrel, and everything else in my view radiated this light. Every particle of light was filled with a palpable, emanating, and amazing love, so soft and beautiful. The power of it was so tangible that I burst into tears and shouted out loud, "Oh, my God, this is paradise, and we've made it into something else!"

For the first time in my life, I saw the true beauty of this world. I began to sob from the pulsating love I saw all around. I realized in an instant that we humans were given

the gift of living on this planet to do something great. We were given this gift of paradise.

My God, I thought, *what have we done? We have so polluted the air, water, and soil. All of nature has suffered in our ignorance.* I saw how we were given free will, and it was our choice to make the earth a paradise or a living hell. It was our choice. Everything had been given to us: The sun, the moon, the stars, water, fire, air, wood, soil, flowers, minerals, fruits, vegetables, trees, animals to keep us company, and birds to sing us songs. And what had our relentless ego and ignorance caused us to do with it?

I could not believe how blind I had been before. How could I have lived this long and not truly seen the beauty of the world in this way? How could I not have understood the gift of this planet? Having been born into this world, I had taken it for granted. The sight of all this and my instant understanding had me sobbing all over again. But instead of crying in despair, I was crying out of a love filled with gratitude. I wanted to apologize to nature, to the animals and flowers and trees for abusing them with my neglect and ignorance of their innate, loving, and divine nature. I understood that animals were pure unconditional love; how could they be otherwise?

I went back into the house, overwhelmed by what had been revealed to me. The compassion I felt for humanity and all of nature was unlike anything I had ever before experienced. The power of the love I felt inside shook my body and mind to its very foundation, and I had a difficult time containing it. Everywhere I looked, I saw only love, I felt only love, and I thought only love. Every cell in my body continued to vibrate with love. I felt like a huge tuning fork that had been struck with divine love, as it reverberated in my entire being. I felt alive with love.

I made my way back into the living room and collapsed onto the couch in a state of loving grace. Instantly, I fell into a deep sleep. When I awoke, I found a new sense of peace. What had happened to me? What miracle had just occurred?

In an effort to get my bearings, I went to the back door and looked out again. This time there was just green grass, flowers, and the apple tree. There was no more shimmering light. My "normal" sight may have returned, but my understanding had changed forever. A new day was dawning for me. All the days of the rest of my life would be changed, for I had stepped out of the deep sleep of ego ignorance onto the path of enlightenment.

This was the day of my spiritual awakening, which would continue to unfold over the years in ways I could never have imagined.

Life after Awakening

In the days that followed, I wondered why I had the visitation from Jesus. Was it just for me, or was I meant to share it?

I felt different inside. I felt more love, and more alive and aware of what was going on around me. Before, I had felt so separate from people and defensive; now I was more relaxed and open. And something else happened that was miraculous. It seemed that Jesus had removed a "veil of ignorance" from my eyes, and opened my inner eye of understanding, compassion, and knowing. I could truly see and comprehend things about other people: I could see others' troubles when I looked at them, their emotional wounds and the corresponding patterns of compensation they had built up over the years. I felt that compensation in the way

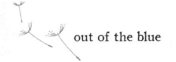

a person used words and by the look in their eyes. I could literally feel if they were telling the truth or trying to conceal something. If they were trying to conceal something, the energy of the words would feel stuck in my solar plexus; if they were truthful, the energy would flow through me. I could only imagine that this was what people meant when they said, "I had a gut feeling."

At first, I was quite shocked by all of this. What before had confused me about other people's behavior now seemed so obvious, and I could easily discern why they acted the way they did. I saw their unresolved suffering so clearly that it was sometimes disturbing to me. I felt privy to feelings that were hidden behind their demeanor. I understood that what I saw of their troubles was just a reflection of the issues they were dealt in life. In other words, it was not the real them; it was just their ego story. The real them was the pure divine light I could see in their eyes.

My new understandings also required that I continually correct my own thoughts and actions. When I was critical of another, whether in thought or out loud, I would feel immediately unsettled inside myself, as I was aware now that I was acting out of the reactive ego state of mind. I realized that much had been given to me, and much would be expected in return. I would be required to live up to my new understandings; I had to put them into practice on a daily basis.

I marveled at all that had happened. And yet I still had to deal with the mundane world—bills needed to be paid, and my daughter needed to be fed, clothed, and loved. Integrating all of this was a challenge, and I still struggled with so many issues. For example, I couldn't help but feel like a dismal failure regarding Deborah. I loved her so much, and yet the knowledge that I could not give her an intact home life with a mother and a father still haunted me, perhaps because I had so yearned for it for myself.

When I went into work at the hospital a few days after Jesus's visitation, I felt so open. I felt so much love for perfect strangers I saw on the street. It was a thrilling feeling unlike anything I had ever experienced. I was like a kid with a new toy. But this was much better, as no one could take it away from me!

My co-workers noticed that something had happened to me—they said I looked different and wondered if I had gotten a new haircut or something. I said nothing. A month later, my boss said in an informal conversation among co-workers, "Oh, Mary's discovered love." I was so astounded but didn't say anything. She could see that something had happened and even named it love. But it was so much more than that . . . it was God.

I also had to get used to being inside myself in a whole new way, since I was able to see and appreciate my own and other people's problems. Before, I'd spent a lot of time judging others; now I had a feeling of compassion toward others and myself. I became a kinder person. I found myself wishing the best for people who were struggling with life, as I too was struggling.

I didn't speak to anyone about my awakening. I felt they would think I was crazy, so I kept it all to myself. Life continued for me, but I had a larger perspective than before and a greater appreciation that there was more to life than met the eye. The poem "The Odes of Solomon," from Stephen Mitchell's book *The Enlightened Heart*, truly speaks to my experiences: It begins with describing how one day grace will fill your heart, transforming you into a being of love, giving you a divine eye. I urge you to sit with this poem for a while. It is truly beautiful.

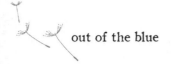

I began reading a lot of books on spirituality, such as the Tao Te Ching and many of Alice Bailey's works like *Esoteric Healing.* I read Shirley MacLaine's *Out on a Limb,* which really hit home. I felt out on a limb, all right. Unable to express or hold my awakening in some familiar context, I kept what was happening inside a secret. In spite of that, people could tell that something was different, and they continued to comment about it in rather surprising ways.

I was in my last year of massage school. Classes were scheduled on weekends with two weeklong retreats each year, which meant that students got to know each other very well. Very shortly after the awakening, during a sharing group at one of the retreats, a classmate burst into tears and yelled at me, "You have so much light pouring out of you I can hardly stand it!" I was stunned and didn't know what to say. This was all new to me as well; I didn't know how to explain what had happened. Others in the group said, "Yeah, you look different. You're more relaxed or something."

Another woman in the group, who was usually kind to me, suddenly became very abrupt in our interactions. In a telephone conversation a few days after I returned home, she explained her behavior. She said, "I could see that something happened to you, and I wanted it, too. That's why I was so nasty to you." I wish I could have explained to her at the time what had happened, but frankly I didn't have the words for it.

I was quite affected by these reactions, which made me feel more than ever that I did not want to share my experiences. I didn't know how to *be* anymore. I needed to learn how to integrate all the inner changes, and solitude became a comforting friend.

It would take a long time for me to adjust to my new eyes and new understandings. I told no one—not my family, not friends at school, not my therapist. I was still in therapy trying to sort out my life, but I never once spoke of these experiences. I had never heard anyone else speaking about these kinds of experiences, so I thought I'd be misunderstood.

Life continued with its challenges. Things did not really get easier; I just had a better perspective on what was happening. Instead of immediately reacting to whatever someone might say or do, I would reflect more on what was going on and respond more calmly. Of course, this didn't happen every time—I would fall back to my reactive ways more times than not. Yet I always came back to the truth of love; I was no longer caught up in the web of ignorance. I now knew that God was at work in all things and all people, and my behavior needed to reflect that knowledge.

Sometimes I would feel that life was more difficult being awake because now I couldn't blame other people for how my life was going. At other times, I was so grateful for being awakened from the suffering that came from thinking, *I'm a failure, life has no meaning, and God is dead!* Knowing the deep love that existed in everyone and in everything also brought me comfort and hope.

In the meantime, I was exploring alternative healing therapies like Reiki. Reiki is a form of energy healing where the practitioner channels energy into the chakra centers of the body by placing their hands over the centers. Since this form of energy treatment seemed to help me so much, I decided to take a workshop and incorporate this form of healing into my massage treatments when practicing on other students at the school. A few days after completing the Reiki course, I had another remarkable experience.

Miraculous Experiences with Sparrows

I was out one afternoon riding my bicycle and stopped alongside the road to briefly watch some kids playing softball. As I was standing over my bike, with one foot on the pavement for balance and the other still on a pedal, for some reason I looked down at the ground. There, within inches of my foot, was a wounded sparrow. Only one of his wings seemed to be working, and he was going around in circles trying to get off the ground.

Without thinking, I scooped him up in my hand and held him next to my heart, hoping the sound of my heartbeat might calm him. Off I went on my bike, heading home. I wasn't really sure what I was going to be able to do for the sparrow, but I couldn't leave him on the ground to die.

Once I got home, I found a cardboard box, emptied it out, and placed the bird inside. He didn't attempt to move very much, partly out of fright, I'm sure, and partly because of his wound. I could see that one of his eyes was severely damaged due to some kind of trauma. I thought for sure this bird was going to die. What was I going to do?

I put some water in a small bowl and got some grass from outside to line the box. Then I called a friend who had sent me to the Reiki classes. "Oh," she said with a laugh, "birds especially get attracted to people who open up to the Reiki energy. Give him some Rescue Remedy, and hold him in your hands and give him Reiki." Rescue Remedy is a combination of flower essences in a liquid suspension said to bring calmness and healing during stress.

After hanging up the phone, I didn't know what to think. Really, I thought my friend was a little goofy. But what did I have to lose? I did Reiki on the bird as instructed and fed him some of the remedy; later, I went to the

store to get some birdseed. I never expected that sparrow to live, but I did Reiki on him a few times a day over the next two days. Every time I came home from work, I rushed to the box, certain I would find a dead sparrow.

On the third day, I came home as usual and went to the box. It was empty! *Oh no,* I thought, *the bird got out of the box and is dead somewhere in a corner.* I went searching for the bird and, much to my shock, he was perched on a chair in the living room! I could not believe my eyes. He started flying around the room. *How could this be? He had been so injured.* It was a miracle. I was totally astounded and amazed.

Now that the bird had recovered, the next task was to release him outside—but how? First I had to catch him. And how would I do that? I brought his box into the living room, where I found him perched again on the chair. I decided to talk to the bird, all the while wondering if that would really work. "Look," I said out loud, "you've got to fly over here to this box. If you do and you let me catch you, I'll release you outside. Don't worry, I won't hurt you."

To my utter and complete astonishment, the bird flew over and perched on the box! With one calm, swift motion, I gently picked him up in my hand and walked to the back door. I looked at him and saw that he still had only one eye to see with, but at least the wound of the injured eye had closed over. I walked down the stairs off the back porch, stood under the apple tree, and released him.

What a sight! I opened my hands and watched him fly to one of the lower branches of the tree. He flew so strongly. I could feel myself choking back tears, and finally just let myself cry. I wished him well and felt such a powerful love between us. He perched for a while on the branch and looked at me, as if to say a final good-bye, then swiftly flew away to another tree next door. His wing had completely

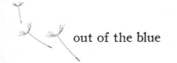

h*ealed, and* he seemed to navigate just fine with his one eye.

In that moment, I felt that the bird and I had communicated our love and appreciation of each other using telepathy. When I went inside, I looked up the word telepathy in a dictionary. It was defined as "the supposed sending of messages from one mind to another by some means other than by speaking or seeing."

*My experience with birds was not_over yet. The very next morning, just as I was about to open the door to the back porch to leave for work, there was a p*igeon standing right in front of it, waiting to get into my house! I thought, What on earth does he want? Did he get a referral from the sparrow? Could my friend have been right about birds sensing this healing energy? I shooed him away a little, so he wouldn't come into my kitchen. He moved away to the other side of the porch but wouldn't leave. That's when I realized he was ill.

I wasn't sure what to do, so I decided to go back in the house and call animal control. They seemed rather perplexed when I tried to explain how the bird wanted to come into my house because he was ill, but they promised to come over and take care of the situation. In the meantime, I had to go to work. I don't know what ever happened to the pigeon, but I stopped doubting my friend and what she had to say about birds being attracted to the Reiki energy.

Experiences with sparrows would continue—curiously, it was only with sparrows, except for that one visit from the pigeon on the back porch. A few years later, when I was at a meditation retreat, I had another astounding experience. In the early morning, I was walking out onto an open-air porch with some friends. There were tables and chairs scattered around where people ate breakfast. I noticed a few sparrows sitting on tabletops eating the last of some crumbs. My friends walked ahead of me to find a table. The sparrows immediately flew away, all except one. Everyone else was on the other end of the porch, but I was lagging behind because I'd noticed the sparrow. He sat on top of the table, and we just looked at one another with great interest.

As we stared at each other, everything seemed to go into slow motion. I knew I could put my finger out and he would sit on it. Slowly, I lowered my right hand to the sparrow's feet with my finger acting as a perch. He hopped on effortlessly! With the sparrow safely sitting on my finger, I brought him up to my eye level. We stared at each other very intently. I was in awe; I think he was as well. The world seemed to stand still. I almost felt like he was going to "talk" to me.

Just at that moment, one of my friends noticed this and walked over while *stretching her hand out, say*ing she also wanted to hold the bird. As she did, he flew away. Then time returned to normal speed and my friend apologized for interrupting. She looked at me rather strangely, as if to say, What the heck are you doing? No one else in the group had noticed what happened.

As I mentioned, before he flew away, I felt that the sparrow was about to communicate something telepathically. Perhaps he could sense I wouldn't hurt him. Perhaps he knew of the incident that had happened with the other sparrow a few years back. I remembered hearing once that every action we performed and every word we spoke was recorded in our consciousness. Did the sparrow sense that? I don't know, but I found the whole experience profoundly moving.

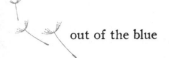

Another time, I was sitting with my eyes closed, meditating on a bench in the lobby of a large building, when I heard the sound of a sparrow. I opened my eyes and noticed there was one sitting on the limb of an indoor ficus tree. I knew that if he didn't somehow get outside, he would die. As I approached him, I told him I wouldn't hurt him and if he would just be still, I would carry him outside. To my astonishment, he let me do just that! I took him in my hands and placed him near my heart, then brought him outside to some nearby hedges, where he quickly took flight. A man had noticed this, and he looked at me with an amazed smile on his face. I smiled back and went inside to finish my meditation, while contemplating what had just happened. By now I felt I had a way with birds (or at least sparrows).

It seemed that this deeper connection with sparrows and nature was a direct result of my spiritual awakening. I no longer held the concept of separateness between nature and me. I could feel on a cellular level that I was in nature and nature was in me. I felt we belonged to a continuum of life rather than as separate unrelated components. I realized that anything done to nature would also have an impact on me, and vice versa.

it's god again

I continued to contemplate my revelatory visit from Jesus. I was still processing being awakened to a whole new energy system in my body, and to a whole new way of seeing, thinking, and feeling. My egoic, emotional walls of defensiveness continued to crumble day by day. These walls had been built to survive my childhood and the years that followed, and it was now time for them to come down. Because, instead of protecting me, they had imprisoned me.

I graduated from massage school, and had hoped to go on and learn more there as an apprentice teacher. However, there were many feelings of discontent between my class and the school, and other members of my class and I were not invited to return. In the past, I would have been completely devastated by something like that. It's not that my feelings weren't hurt—I was in fact deeply hurt—but I was more accepting of the situation than I previously would have been. The act of being more accepting of a disappointment was an achievement for me, and allowed me to be more open to moving on instead of wallowing in my loss.

Nevertheless, I cried almost every day as a way to release tears that needed to be shed. As time passed and life presented new opportunities, I realized that I wouldn't have been open to them if I had stayed at the school.

Einstein's Theory of Relativity

I spent a great deal of time by myself in nature, sitting outside in silence; this silence allowed me to experience nature more acutely.

Still cleansing emotionally, I visited a state park that has a beach filled with huge boulders, which seem to have been there from the beginning of time. As I sat on one of the rocks, I began to feel its innate nature—solid, reliable, constant, and even wise. I realized that these rocks had been there for thousands of years and had been silent witnesses to all the comings and goings of the ages. Many people had sat on them with all their troubles and life stories, just like me, yet these rocks remained neither disturbed nor elated. They simply sat in their peaceful state; nothing shook them. I thought I should be more like a rock—solid, stable, and content—during the inevitable ups and downs of life.

I remembered my experience of the light particles when I looked out at my backyard, and I realized that these rocks were also made of the same kind of particles. I really wanted to understand what had happened to me with the light; I wanted to better understand my experience with Jesus. I was less identified with having only a physical body, as now I knew I also had a light body.

The closest intellectual concept I could equate with my experience of the light and my physical body was Einstein's theory of relativity: $E=mc^2$, energy equals mass times the speed of light squared. I felt that this equation somehow related to my experience of having a physical body *and* a light body at the same time—but how? How did this matter I called my physical body relate to the light and to God and science? I wanted a scientific explanation to comprehend in my mind what I knew to be true in my heart, that love and light were all.

I also began to use the phrase *energy medicine* to describe my own healing process. Working with the energy of the body through massage, Reiki, and acupuncture was a field of medicine I felt could truly help people heal. But in the mid-1980s, not many understood this as deeply as I had experienced it.

I wished I could find someone who could explain all this to me. I wasn't quite sure what it was I so longed to see in another—perhaps it was a kind of wisdom. As I mentioned before, one of the most remarkable effects after Jesus's revelations was that my eyes were cleared, so I could see things that were troubling people. I yearned to find a clear pair of eyes in another, but was unable to do so.

Life continued to change, and I was downsized out of my job at the hospital during an administrative reorganization, but was happy to leave because I really didn't like being there anymore. I received a little severance pay to keep me going, and my practice as a massage therapist began to grow.

In early May 1986, I happened to see an advertisement for a free lecture entitled "Energy Medicine." This concept had been on my mind for a while now, and I looked forward to the lecture with great anticipation. The ad said there would be a panel of practitioners who would talk about the energy in the body: an acupuncturist, a chiropractor, a

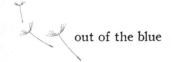

medical doctor who had studied the efficacy of acupuncture in China, and an energy bodyworker. I attended the lecture to see if what they had to say might give me a better understanding of my spiritual experiences. What occurred next riveted my attention and changed my life in a way I could not have imagined.

As each person on the panel stood to speak, they stated their name and introduced themselves, all except one. The energy bodyworker stood up and said, "$E=mc^2$, Einstein's theory of relativity. Einstein proved that matter, energy, and the speed of light are related." He went on to explain how the physical body was made of matter, and was energy as a dense temporary expression. He said that the light energy that gave the body life was matter in its most refined expression. He further said that everything was made of energy, and that light, energy, and matter were inextricably linked. He explained that matter was essentially only a transformation of light energy.

I couldn't believe it! Here was the answer to my question about Einstein's theory and its relation to my experiences. A sense of urgency took over my entire being. I ran up to this man as soon as there was a break, grabbed his arm, and said, "I must see you." I made an appointment to meet with him for a healing session a few days later.

Another turning point in my life was about to occur . . . something extraordinary and transformational was about to happen. On the day of the appointment with the healer, I would also meet someone else who would change my life. This meeting was preordained; I was about to meet my destiny. This meeting would clearly be a continuation of my visitation with Jesus two years prior. Through this person, I would come to understand so much more of what Jesus had imparted. Grace was about to enter my life again, very powerfully, and impact me forever.

Finding a Pair of Clear Eyes

I counted the days until the healing session, intensely curious as to what might happen. Finally, the day came. When I walked into the healer's office, we said a polite hello, and he excused himself for a minute to speak with someone in the other room. While he was gone, I found myself staring at a picture hanging on the wall. To say I was riveted would be an understatement—I felt drawn to that picture like a moth to a flame.

It was a picture of a woman's face, and as I looked into her seemingly endless eyes, I heard myself saying out loud, "I know her and she knows me." I had a flash in my mind of a lifetime I had spent as a monk with this person, and I knew it had been a very happy lifetime. I heard her telepathically say that we were coming together again to complete something. As I searched her eyes in the picture, I realized that they seemed to go on forever and knew everything about energy and truth. Yes, I had found the clear eyes I had been looking for! But who was this? And what did it all mean?

Just then the healer walked into the room. I repeated, "I know her and she knows me." Then I asked him, "Who is that, anyway? Is she alive? She knows everything there is to know about energy and truth."

"That could be. Yes, she's alive. Do you want to meet her? She'll be in Boston in two weeks."

"Yeah, I want to meet her. Is she a monk?"

"Yes," he said. He told me that he'd be in touch when she arrived.

I was thrilled by the possibility of meeting this woman. I wondered if this meant that she and I were to continue the spiritual teachings from the time I had been her monk in that past life. I secretly hoped it would be true.

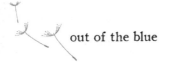

I then noticed a little dog had followed the healer into the room. I was immediately captivated by him, because he looked like the dog I had as a child, a dog that I had to put to sleep after 16 years as my best friend. Upon the sight of him, I started crying and then weeping uncontrollably. I was shocked to realize that I was still holding the incredibly painful memory of losing my dog, of holding her in my arms as the vet put her to sleep with an injection. Apparently these feelings had been buried very deep in a place that seemed inaccessible until this point. As it happened, I was 19 when my dog had died—the same age when I'd found out I was pregnant and had to make arrangements to put my baby up for adoption.

I told the healer about the memory of my dog and my pregnancy, and he began working with my energy right away. At first he just held me as I cried, and told me to breathe deeply and follow my breath. As I did, he made swooshing sounds with his breath that seemed to clear and help move my emotions. I remembered that emotions are energy, and energy could be worked with and transformed. Perhaps he was transmuting the energy of my emotions with his breath.

He then had me lie down on my back on a massage table, and asked me to follow my breath and stay with the emotions. At my request, he had his little dog come up and lie next to me. This was the beginning of the longest healing session I ever had, lasting six hours. I felt as if I were clearing out every deep hurt I had ever felt in this lifetime and in others. Layer after layer came up, and I thought, *Will this ever end?* I knew I wasn't just rehashing the painful events in my life, but releasing and cleansing them from the depths of my soul.

I sobbed and sobbed. To my surprise, at certain times the healer sobbed, too. He seemed to be helping me get the feelings out. At one point, a few hours into the treatment, he said, "I can feel your daughter in your energy field—the one you gave up for adoption. I'm not supposed to tell you. Normally I wouldn't, but I feel drawn to tell you. You have a very strong spiritual connection with her. She wants me to tell you something: She wants me to tell you that she doesn't hate you for giving her up. She understands, and she loves you."

I felt my heart break into thousands of pieces as he said those words. I continued to sob, and so did he—both of us seemed very involved in this healing. A few more hours passed like this, until we finally neared the end of the session. I felt calm and purified from releasing so much.

The healer stood at the end of the table, with his abdomen touching the soles of my feet, and instructed me to breathe slowly. All of a sudden I felt a divine presence: A flood of light began pouring into the top of my head, flowing down through my arms and entire body, down my legs and out my feet. I thought, *It's God again! But why is He here?* It felt like the time Jesus had visited me, only stronger. When I felt this light pour out of my hands and feet, I wondered if the healer felt it, too, but I said nothing.

I thought of the image of Jesus, with light coming from his hands and feet. *Oh,* I thought, *so that's how Jesus healed. He healed using this light.* I envisioned a picture of the blessed Mother Mary and remembered seeing light coming from her hands and feet, too. She had the same divine light as Jesus. I thought of the halos around the heads of saints, and knew that this was the same light.

I felt so peaceful and content, and I wanted this to last forever. The light scintillated inside every cell of my body and ran along every pathway parallel to my nervous system. All these pathways of light, I realized, corresponded with the meridians I had seen on acupuncture charts.

My God, the meridians do exist as light—the Chinese were right! I felt so much love inside me, so much light, and extremely happy and comforted. After a few minutes the experience subsided, and the healer left the room so that I could rest before getting up.

By the time he returned, I was off the table and sitting on the floor. I felt like a rag doll from all the crying but also very light and quite peaceful. As he sat down next to me, he said, "Hail Mary, full of grace." I was curious why he had said that but didn't want to ask, because I felt really protective of my experience with the light and didn't want to get into a conversation about it. I wondered if he could actually feel what I felt. Then he said, "You have a lot of grace coming your way." I thought, *I do? I wonder why he said that.* Still, I said nothing.

I felt so wonderful after the session. I went home and slept more deeply than I had in months.

Meeting My Spiritual Teacher

As promised, the healer called me to meet the monk I had seen in his picture. When I met her, I felt that she was indeed my spiritual teacher, although I'd had no conscious thought of needing one before seeing her picture. I simply wanted to find a pair of eyes—or so I thought. She happened to give a talk on the ego the day I met her. I listened with great interest, and found that what Jesus had said to me two years prior was exactly what she was saying now.

Finally, I had found someone who could completely understand the revelations I'd had with Jesus. It was an enormous relief to me; I felt I could tell her anything and she would completely understand. I knew she'd been my

teacher in a past life and we had come together again to complete something, though I didn't know what that was. I did know for certain that the peace and love I felt in her presence was something I wanted for myself.

Another strange thing happened in the days that followed: I started spontaneously writing spiritual poetry for hours on end. I never had to labor to find the right words; they just seemed to pour into me and through the pen onto the paper. When this happened, I always felt so peaceful and happy. Writing poetry acted as an outlet, a way for me to express the spiritual experiences I had been given.

After meeting my teacher, I learned how to meditate and chant God's name, which brought serenity to my mind. I began reading spiritual scriptures like *The Yoga Sutras of Patanjali, Shankara's Crest-Jewel of Discrimination* (also known as the *Vivekachudamani*), and the Bhagavad Gita. Although these texts were written hundreds of years ago, they are just as relevant today in discovering and understanding our true divine nature while living in the world, and I'd like to share them with you here:

— Patanjali was born in India around 120 B.C. and was considered an *avatar*, a sage, self-realized at birth; a *sutra* is a spiritual discourse. What I remember most from his book was when he said that we must learn to let the soul drive the vehicle of our bodies instead of the ego, as the soul will lead us back to union with our natural state of divinity.

— Shankara was born in India around the 8th century A.D. and became a *sannyasin*, a religious ascetic, as a child. He was known as a great spiritual sage, philosopher, poet, and monk who established a number of monasteries. The *Vivekachudamani* takes the form of a dialogue between the spiritual master and his disciple regarding the soul, the

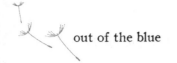

nature of the world, and how to reach self-realization. It's a small and very readable book that I often carried with me.

— The Bhagavad Gita, whose title means "the song of God," is a long dialogue between God, known as Krishna, and Arjuna, the disciple. God answers the disciple's questions on the nature of knowledge, action, wisdom, awareness, devotion, true renunciation, and self-realization.

Later, I came to discover that Henry David Thoreau read the Bhagavad Gita during his stay at Walden Pond, and that very copy is on display at the Concord Museum in Concord, Massachusetts. Albert Einstein, Carl Jung, Dr. Albert Schweitzer, Aldous Huxley, Ralph Waldo Emerson, and many other historically great minds were also united in their praise of the Gita.

Through the practices of chanting and meditation, and by reading these ancient discourses, I learned how to worship myself by meditating on my true divine nature, my soul, with the knowledge that God lived inside me as me. I felt as if a breath of fresh air had entered my life, and that I was on the brink of a new and exciting adventure. It was now June 1986.

Recognizing All of Life as Spiritual

Over the summer, I completely immersed myself in the spiritual practices of meditation, contemplation, and chanting, and in offering service at the meditation center where I had met my teacher. All of these practices felt very natural and familiar.

I traveled to a larger retreat site to see my teacher again, spending a few days in meditation, where I was given a spiritual initiation—an awakening of my consciousness through a transmission of wisdom from my teacher. This made meditation a lot easier, as I could sit down and let my mind rest for a change. Meditation helped me enormously in my life; I felt more focused, balanced, and grounded.

I was certain that meditation had aided me in landing a great job at the Massachusetts Institute of Technology (MIT) by the end of the year, as an administrative assistant managing the office and organizing international conferences for a new department, the Center for Theoretical Geo/Cosmo Plasma Physics. I loved my new boss, who had a pleasant demeanor and even looked like the Dalai Lama. Finally, I'd found a job and a boss I truly enjoyed.

Meditation became something I did during my lunch breaks at work. In the warm weather, I would sit outside in a quiet courtyard. I particularly enjoyed basking in the sunlight among the foliage, while feeding the many sparrows that gathered for my leftovers. Their little faces melted any tension I felt from the morning's work; they were so adorable and full of innocence.

Sparrows perched on the branches of a nearby apple tree that was actually a descendant of the tree Isaac Newton had sat under when an apple fell on his head, inspiring him to understand the laws of gravity. Surrounding myself with beauty and inspiration in this way, my mind quickly settled down into meditation.

During one of these lunches, I had a breakthrough in my practice. Before the breakthrough, a black wall of fear would arise from within as I meditated. I would mentally pull back from it and then stop my meditation. I would begin the meditation again, and again it would happen. After six months of this, something changed; I was finally able to break through this fear. On that day, the black wall appeared as always, but instead of moving away from it,

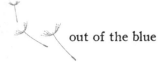

I finally had the courage to move *toward* it. As I did, the wall of fear disappeared like a fog, and I emerged into a shining light. I could hardly believe it! The light was so bright, and I felt immediately peaceful. Never again would I encounter that wall of fear. My self-effort was rewarded with a greater sense of inner peace in my meditations and throughout my daily activities.

I also offered service in the form of cooking, cleaning, and administrative skills at the local meditation center. I noticed that no matter what service I offered, I always felt remarkably happy afterward. How could cleaning toilets make someone feel so joyful? The mystery of service as a spiritual practice always amazed me. My mind would transform negative thoughts to positive ones as I performed the most mundane tasks. Any gloom from the day would disappear; it simply melted away without me even thinking about it.

And then there was chanting, which combined music and singing with sacred mantras that vibrated at the highest level of consciousness. I had sung in choirs in my youth and adult years, so this immediately felt like a familiar practice. In the past, singing had always put me in a good mood, but chanting seemed to have a more powerful energy. During the chant and afterward, I'd gain a clearer perspective on whatever problems I was experiencing in my life—cares would just melt from my mind and heart. For example, I would get answers to questions, like how to handle difficult situations at work or how to solve an organizational problem. Chanting also gave my mind greater focus, and I accomplished more at work in a shorter time.

When I first began these spiritual practices, I felt as if I were living two lives: a worldly life and a spiritual life. But the more I did the practices, the more I realized that there was only one life and all life was sacred and spiritual. Washing dishes could be just as spiritual as praying—it was all in one's attitude. I became aware of my actions as an expression of love; it was a little shift, but it made a world of difference in how I felt inside.

I discovered that everything in my life could be an offering, and little things counted the most: a kind word to a stranger, holding a door open for the next person, letting someone go ahead of me in line at the grocery store when they had only one item. I understood that God lived in the details of life, and it was how I lived the details that seemed to make all the difference. I noticed that I was becoming a kinder and gentler person, slowly but surely.

Still, life was not without its challenges, as I continued to grow emotionally and spiritually. My ego was quite strong in the form of self-judgment, pride, and a critical approach to things. I also tended to be an impatient person, and came to understand that this stemmed from an underlying anxiety that played out in rushing around to get as much done as possible in the shortest amount of time. I realized at some point that I could still get things done in an efficient manner without rushing. In order to change the habit, I needed to look at the root of the underlying anxiety. The pride, negativity, and impatience needed to be confronted—I needed to face down all these impostors and find the real me, the loving me.

Part of facing these impostors was having the willingness to look at myself honestly and say, *Yes, I am like that, aren't I?* When I did this, any resistance to change would melt away, along with the mental habits. I recognized that these negative mental habits were not the real me, the divine me; they were the companions of the ego, which could not live in the face of scrutiny and self-inquiry. Even though this process was very challenging, I felt so much

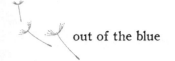

better at the end of each spiritual growth spurt, as if I had unburdened myself from many lifetimes of suffering. It seemed I had become a student of meditation, chanting, service, and self-inquiry, and I loved it!

Little did I know that all of this inner and outer immersion in the spiritual practices was a preparation for what was to come. Little did I know that I was about to experience the most awesome event of my life. This experience would change me yet again in the most profound ways, and would even foretell what awaited all humanity.

What happened to me was so extraordinary, I never could have imagined it.

CHAPTER 5

self-realization

Two years passed, filled with dedication and devotion to my spiritual practices. In the summer of 1988, I decided to take some time away from home to attend a retreat. I very much enjoyed studying and contemplating the teachings of the spiritual masters, so I signed up for a course at the retreat site. I also yearned to be with my teacher, who had just returned after being away for two years.

It was a beautiful day in early July. I was sitting outside by myself on the retreat grounds during a lunch break. In my mind, I was repeating some words that had been given by my teacher during the course as a way to clear old, negative mental habits. At the same time, I was reading from *The Light of the Soul,* a paraphrase of *The Yoga Sutras of Patanjali* with commentary by Alice Bailey. The book said that the ego-personality-mind must be replaced by the soul as the driver of the physical vehicle, the body. I wondered what it would be like not to be driven by my ego-personality-mind, to simply let it melt into my soul and allow my soul to lead the way. I found this a totally fascinating concept and was utterly captivated

by it. I had full faith that what I was thinking about could happen, and would possibly even happen to me.

Just then, as I sat quietly under the shade of a huge pine tree, the most wondrous thing happened! It was simply astonishing, and at the same time it seemed like the most natural thing in the world. What I am about to recount is the ultimate experience in any human life. This experience gave me the understanding as to why I kept coming back to this earth, lifetime after lifetime.

Fully engrossed in the book and deep in contemplation, I suddenly felt a presence come over me like a huge cloud. It hovered over my head and began to shower me with a golden light, which felt like the sweetest nectar I have ever experienced.

This golden light came down over my head and shoulders, and I knew in a flash that this was God, Brahman, the ultimate reality, the source of all that exists! In the past I had only named the feeling of divine presence as "God," but now I also experienced it as "Brahman"—a divine ultimate reality existing inside me, as well as outside as a creation of the world. (Note that I use both names, although I felt them as interchangeable.)

Reclaiming Our Divinity

So many things began to happen all at once, as God/Brahman spoke these exact words:

> *Here is your divinity,*
> *the divinity that awaits all mankind.*
> *Your soul wants full expression now.*
> *This is the presence.*
> *This is the living presence.*
> *This is living. This is real.*

It was a voice unlike any I'd ever heard before. It was male-sounding, yet it seemed beyond any quality of maleness in the humans I had known. This pure God/Brahman voice was very soft, divinely healing, and completely consoling. This presence poured over me like liquid light, like a golden nectar, and I immediately became deeply peaceful.

As God/Brahman spoke each sentence, different experiences and understandings automatically awakened inside me, the very same way it had with Jesus, only this time more powerfully. As God/Brahman said, "Here is your divinity, the divinity that awaits all mankind," my heart leapt with joy that divinity could and did indeed belong to all humanity. I remembered Jesus teaching that the kingdom of God is within, but I had no idea that *this* was what he meant!

The degree of divinity was awesome to experience. The sheer divine power was unbelievable! I thought, *This lives inside every human being? How amazing. So much divine power! How could this be?* Yet I knew beyond any shadow of doubt that it was true. And when God/Brahman spoke of "the divinity that awaits all mankind," it was clear that it was mankind's destiny to reclaim it. I likened our hidden divinity to having a blanket covering a piece of furniture: The furniture was still there, but you couldn't see it because the blanket was over it—but if you peeled back the blanket, there it was. I understood that our ego-personality-mind was covering our divinity like a blanket.

I knew with absolute conviction that we were here to reclaim our divinity. I knew I had come back to this earth to rediscover it as a permanent state of consciousness and awareness. For so long, for so many lifetimes, I had become used to having an ego-personality-mind as my identity, convinced in every lifetime that the particular person and role I played was the real me. I had always thought I was a

particular person, nothing more, nothing less. How could it have been otherwise? I didn't know any other way— I didn't know anything else was possible. Even now that I did know what was possible, I still could hardly believe such a thing was true! But here I was, living the indisputable truth, the greatest truth of human existence: divinity.

I hadn't had any concept of this enormous omniscience living within a human body, so to say it was astounding is an understatement. Truly, words cannot contain or express what was revealed to me. I kept thinking, *Oh, my God, so this is what Jesus, the saints, Buddha, Ramakrishna, Confucius, and all the great ones were talking about. Oh, my God . . . oh, my God!* I was amazed, elated, and buoyantly joyous! The power, bliss, and ecstasy that surged through every cell in my being made me feel very, very happy and completely whole. I was filled with the wisdom of the Ancient Ones. I *was* the wisdom of the Ancient Ones, and so is all humanity. I realized that it was our time to lay claim to our divine inheritance and knowledge of the truth within.

Unity Consciousness as God/Brahman

When God/Brahman stated, "This is the presence. This is the living presence," I felt the light energy filter down my body, inside and out. When it reached the bottom of my spine, all the energy started traveling back up to my head. I had heard of the *kundalini,* the spiritual energy that rests at the lowest chakra at the end of the spine, but now I was experiencing it in all its fullness! As it started moving up my spine, it felt like a carpet of energy rolling up—taking with it all my fears, all my physical sexual desires, all my psychological needs for others to support me, all my feelings of separation, and all my concerns of life as this individual person. All the issues that worried my ego-personality-mind were being rolled up in that energy, along with the script of life as Mary.

This energy took up everything in its wake until it finally reached the space between my eyebrows. There, something seemed to open with divine permission, and the kundalini energy went farther, to the very top of my head. All of a sudden I had the thought, the experience, and the complete, total understanding: *Aham Brahmasmi! I am Brahman! I am God, I am God!* I no longer felt, *I am Mary with such-and-such a life.* Now I knew beyond any doubt that I was God!

With that, a flood of golden-nectar light flowed like a continuous waterfall from the heavens down into the chakra located at the top of my head, which opened to greet it. I had remembered that spiritual masters were sometimes referred to as "the fountainhead." I was now experiencing the source of this fountainhead: God.

The waterfall of light rushed from my head chakra to my heart, and all of a sudden, my heart chakra burst open. The light poured out of my heart, like water gushing from a huge fire hose. Immediately, I felt my entire energy field spreading out, expanding in all directions about a hundred yards. The light felt like an ocean of pure compassion, pouring out of my heart in an unceasing flow.

I knew in that moment I had become God/Brahman! In that instant recognition of my Godness, I experienced a state of unity consciousness. As I looked out upon all I could see, the feeling was, *I am Brahman, and all this is my creation.* I knew the awareness of being God/Brahman was the only true existence, that all things came from God/Brahman. In this state, I felt completely one, without any feeling of separateness. There was no me and God/

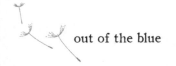

Brahman, there was *only* God/Brahman. My single identity as Mary had been absorbed into my true essence and the essence of everything: God/Brahman.

To have this experience was also to be given the divine knowledge that went with it. Unity consciousness felt like my natural state; it simply was me. I understood that being Mary was a role I'd taken on that fit the ego-personality-mind, while the essence of who I truly am was divine consciousness. It felt natural and normal to be in a divine state of contentment, bliss, perfection, and unity. It felt more natural than being in the state of the fearful, ego-driven personality-mind, which felt like a terrible suffering, a personal hell. Divinity felt like home, and I was elated to finally be back, existing here in this physical body as God/Brahman. This was the truth of who I was. This was the truth of all humanity. This was the truth beyond religion. This was what was before religion even came into being.

Further, I understood that I was experiencing eternity because I had no beginning and no end, existing as this divine ever-unfolding bliss of God/Brahman consciousness. The immensity of happiness I experienced is very hard to describe. It felt like a new and unfolding bliss from one moment to the next, without end. Oh, joy, unending joy!

I knew beyond any doubt that if anyone had come near me at this moment and touched me, they too would have felt the power of this enormous divine energy. They would have simply been ignited by it! In other words, they would have experienced in their own conscious awareness that they themselves were divine.

I swayed inwardly with a feeling of bliss, the pure ecstasy of knowing I AM. I AM. I AM That I AM. What joy, what peace, what contentment! I felt completely fulfilled. I felt totally pure, beyond any need of outward support and,

therefore, beyond any motive. I understood that this was what the great spiritual masters had discovered for themselves: the truth of their being—God/Brahman. This was what we as humanity were here to discover, as this is what we already are.

I knew that most of us weren't aware of this in our conscious, everyday waking state; rather, most of us were only aware of being a particular person. I understood that humanity was stuck in the dream of the ego-personality-mind and we needed to wake up to our true self, our true nature. The time and opportunity to do so were at hand. This state was our true inheritance, and we needed to lay claim to it.

While I was in this state of ecstasy and Godness, I noticed a glow of golden light surrounding me. I marveled that I could see it, as I knew this light was my true body. The flesh in and of itself looked dead; the light surrounding my physical body was what was alive. The flesh was a temporary physical temple to house this light; it was the light that animated the body and gave it life. All this was astounding, yet feeling and seeing it all seemed so natural. It felt like a remembering. This light energy was indeed "the living presence" and being in this state was indeed "living" and this light of divinity was indeed "real" as God/Brahman had spoken.

I thought again of how this light was what was portrayed as the halo often seen in pictures of saints, surrounding their heads and coming from their hands and feet. I remembered the experience I had with the healer as he was working with his breath; it was the same light that coursed through my body. I realized that we too were saints, and the light inside our physical temples was all the same divine light. Yes, it was true!

I felt alive in a way I had never experienced before. Instead of feeling myself as my physical body and my

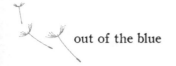

problems, I experienced myself as the light. I was truly *alive as* light. I felt free from all concerns, and that I had come home. I felt completely free from fear—I never realized how much I carried around until I was in this divine state and didn't have it. In fear's place, there was profound, pure, motiveless, divine love and compassion. If I were to act from this place, it would not be from the will of the ego but from pure divine will and love.

I realized that I had crossed over from mere human consciousness belonging to the human kingdom to divine consciousness belonging to the divine kingdom, from where all humanity had originated. We are all saints, in essence, being readied to wake up. It didn't matter what religion one belonged to; this was something that was there before religion and would be there after. Yes, that was my experience. This was the great destiny of humanity, the great destiny waiting to be discovered inside each person. I knew this beyond any doubt.

In comparison, the human state of consciousness I had known for so many years and lifetimes felt like being in exile, like living in a strange world, mixed with so many emotions, desires, distresses, and conflicts. It felt like a terrible suffering; I did not feel at home there. Instead, I had found my true home inside my very own awareness! I had indeed finally come home and felt totally *at* home as God/ Brahman.

In this moment, I realized that all suffering came from being out of union with one's innate divine essence: God/ Brahman. I knew that human consciousness consisted of doubt, fear, pride, jealousy, motive, need, possessiveness, lack, and feeling imperfect and separate. Surely I had suffered those. I also knew that even human kindness and love could be tinged with motives. I reflected on how human consciousness encompassed blame, hatred, and distinctions like "right and wrong" or "good and bad," driven by the ego-personality-mind.

I understood that we must use our human lives to return to our divine state while still living in our physical bodies. I knew beyond any doubt that that was the whole point of our existence—to rediscover and return to our true selves while in the midst of living our lives. We were not meant to go to a mountaintop; we were meant to go inside our consciousness to rediscover and lay claim to the essence and source of that consciousness—divinity, God/Brahman. Then, all sense of suffering would disappear.

My experience of divine consciousness consisted of pure fearlessness, total fulfillment, and a sense of wholeness without need of support. It was beyond the pairs of opposites, such as good and bad. It consisted of the blissful knowledge that we are God/Brahman. It encompassed a divine compassion that ego-driven human consciousness could not know or imagine, for it does not live in ego-driven consciousness.

I likened this awakening of divine consciousness to finding the pot of gold at the end of the rainbow—everyone needs to find the pot of gold at the end of the rainbow inside themselves. I realized that what lay behind this symbolism was the knowledge that the seven main chakras located along our spinal column have a color associated with each of them. These colors comprised the seven colors of the rainbow; we are literally walking rainbows. The pot of gold is the divine light located in the head region, the crown chakra. This crown chakra is where our divinity rests, waiting to be accessed, waiting to be rediscovered and reclaimed by us. It is already present within us—it is present within our human body in the form of light.

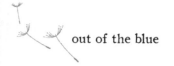

Responsibility of the Human Kingdom

As my experience of divinity continued, I experienced the wisdom and understandings contained in the light. I was given an understanding of the kingdoms: mineral, vegetable, animal, human, and divine. I understood that as humans, it is our duty to rise up and reclaim our divine kingdom through self-realization. We need to realize that we are the great self, God/Brahman, the One living in time but beyond time, the One living in this world but not of this world.

When humans experience self-realization, the other kingdoms will evolve as well. Only the human kingdom is capable of self-realization; the mineral, vegetable, and animal kingdoms do not have this ability. Therefore, all the other kingdoms depend on us to evolve spiritually. We are the caretakers of this earth. It is our responsibility to wake up and reclaim our true home, the divine kingdom within. All things will become like new in the presence of awakened divinity.

I then noticed more fully that physical desire had left me. I hadn't noticed how I'd carried, on a subtle and not-so-subtle level, the physical desire for contact with another human body. It seemed like this desire had a life of its own, as if it were a feeling constantly playing like background music.

I realized that in human relations, intercourse was as close to an instant feeling of bliss that one could have. But it is in no way like the divine state. While enjoying the physical pleasures as a human, one could not imagine that there is something far superior to them. I could not have imagined this myself—but here I was, in a state of total bliss without a trace of physical desire. It felt like such a relief. I felt unimaginably happy and fulfilled.

I thought about how the culmination of physical desire in orgasm was a fleeting moment of physical satisfaction that faded quickly, leaving one wanting more, in an endless cycle of desire and need. Unless one could imagine that there was a way out of this unending desire, into a permanent state of bliss, one would not seek to find it. Such is the power of physical desire. In a very real way, I realized, we don't have physical desires; they have us. We would be enslaved to the satisfaction of our desires until we were freed of the trap of the ego-personality-mind. Clearly, this was how I (and most of humanity) lived.

The divine experience, on the other hand, left me feeling completely enlivened, continuously full, ecstatically complete, and ever new without end. Desire did not exist in the divine inner kingdom, only total fulfillment and unending bliss. I could hardly believe my great fortune. I had made it out of the endless sea of desire and into the kingdom of divinity. I had crossed over! I felt so free . . . I had no idea a person could feel so free. It was a whole other world.

Consciousness Precedes Matter

As I looked across the lawn on this day of self-realization, I noticed the leaves, the buildings, the dirt, indeed the very air, sparkling like diamonds. I could see tiny particles of light in each, reminding me of the experience I'd had in my backyard in 1984. This scintillating light was in everything, everywhere I looked. But now, I understood in a much deeper way that everything in this world was made of consciousness, whether animate or inanimate, and this consciousness is what creates matter. In other words, consciousness preceded matter, and this consciousness was divine light, divinity itself, God/Brahman made manifest

as the world. This was the experience sages, mystics, and saints had spoken of so many times. And now, in this moment, I knew it as truth.

I saw some people walking along the sidewalk, crossing from one building to the next, and I could hardly believe my eyes! Hovering just above each of their foreheads was an oval-shaped disk of light, and light particles flowed down from them and over each person like a shower of snowflakes. They reminded me of walking Christmas trees, with the lighted star at the top and light draping down over the tree. I had an urge to shout, "Look! Look just above your eyes, it's your soul! Can't you see it?" But I knew that even if I shouted, they wouldn't be able to see it. I wanted so much for them to see it, though. I was in a rapturous state of divinity. I felt so fulfilled, so complete, so satisfied, so immensely happy, and totally grateful.

I knew that this was my true state, and yet I could remember the state of living in the ego-personality-mind. It didn't feel like living at all; it felt like the walking dead. When God/Brahman said, "This is the living presence. This is living. This is real," I understood these words as a direct experience. This was indeed true living.

All my suffering—all emotional, spiritual, mental, and physical pain—had left me, along with desire and fear. There was nothing else to achieve, nothing else to strive for. I was elated and also completely aware of my surroundings. I wasn't spaced out or unable to function. In fact, I was more present than I had ever been in my life and acutely aware of everything going on around me, as I was one with all of it. I felt so completely grounded, whole, and unafraid. It was the most relaxing state I had ever experienced. I was home at last. *My God,* I thought, *I didn't even know this place existed inside me.* Heaven was indeed inside me, in my consciousness, which filled my body, my temple. I kept thanking God/Brahman; finally, no more suffering!

Living on this earth, I had known a lot about suffering, either experiencing it myself or reading or hearing about others'. I had always accepted that human beings would suffer one way or the other, that it was a part of life. I had no idea that one could actually live in this world without suffering.

No one had told me of the bliss of the self—no one had ever told me that bliss was our *true* state. Most of humanity was convinced that we could only live in the human realm, in the human state of consciousness, belonging to human beings and human suffering, with God being somewhere else. But on this day I knew we were more than human beings; we were divinity itself. I knew that suffering would eventually leave with the dawn of our divinity, in the same way darkness gives way to the rising sun.

A New Day Is Dawning for Humanity

As I looked across the lawn now, I saw what could only be called a vision. About 30 feet off the ground, a cloud appeared, and Jesus stood in the middle, his hands and eyes lifted toward the heavens. The cloud along with Jesus began ascending until it disappeared. *Oh,* I wondered, *have I ascended as well? Is this the ascension we are all to make, from human consciousness to divine consciousness?* I felt this was true.

That day was a shattering one for me. All of my concepts of people, life, suffering, and God were completely blown apart, with no trace of recognition. On that day, I

saw the greatness of humanity. I experienced "the divinity that awaits all mankind," and nothing would ever be the same for me. All of my judgments, and criticisms of others and myself, were annihilated. No longer could I judge anyone and let myself get away with it. Divinity lived in everyone and everything, so who was there to judge, who was there to criticize? This divinity was void of any kind of exclusiveness; it belonged to everyone, everywhere, equally, without judgment or measure. To behave or believe otherwise would be to deny our very own existence.

I truly knew that a new opportunity was being revealed and offered for humanity. It was nothing short of astonishing. It was real and it was big. I felt that the end of our limited existence, as we knew it, was coming. For thousands of years, the masses of humanity had been suffering and living under the weight of the ego-personality-mind. We had been in a long sleep regarding our true, normal state—but a new day would come with the dawning of our divinity. I knew with certainty that each of us, if we wanted and if we chose, could wake up to this.

My experience of divinity continued as I watched people walking by. Not only could I see their divinity pouring over and into their physical bodies, I also saw their struggles to be free, their issues and concerns. I thought, *Do they know they are God in the midst of these struggles?*

I also felt enormous love for each person. It was difficult to describe the kind of love I felt. It had none of the human impurities such as lust, possessiveness, infatuation, attachment, or jealousy; it loved because its nature was love. It was an unsullied love.

Returning to Ego

I looked down at my watch and saw that it was time to go help with the lunch dishes as part of my service while staying at the retreat. What an interesting situation: There I was in the state of divinity, knowing I was God/Brahman, and I needed to do the dishes!

I realized that our state was the thing that made all the difference while living in human form. We didn't just sit around doing nothing when we became self-realized; we still functioned, but we functioned in continual joy. In fact, it didn't matter what we were doing in this state of bliss, as it didn't come and go but remained what it was. We didn't lose our minds in all this; we gained our divinity and functioned with greater clarity and concern for the welfare of others.

As I got up to walk to the dish room, I knew I was experiencing the highest state a human could reach. There was nothing else for me to attain—this was it. This knowing continued to overwhelm me with gratitude and an enormous peace.

I stood in the dish room in front of a huge tub filled with soapsuds and dirty dishes, and wondered what effect my state had on those around me who were also washing up. As I had that thought, I glanced up, and a woman across from me looked directly at me. As our eyes met, she burst into tears. I quickly looked down into the soapy dishwater as I heard her sobs. The force of this God love was so palpable inside my body, she'd felt it when I looked at her. I knew as she sobbed that this love inside me had touched that source of love within her—her tears were tears of longing for the divinity living inside herself. I finished the dishes in silence and kept my eyes on the soapsuds.

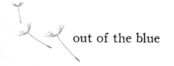

out of the blue

As I walked out of the dish room some 20 minutes later, I wasn't prepared for what happened next. I noticed that my state of total union with God/Brahman was beginning to slip. Someone stopped to ask me a question, and the first feeling I experienced was fear! I quickly answered their question and left the building, feeling the veil of fear closing over my state of total blissful union with God/Brahman. My old ego-driven personality state, with all of its feeling of lack, was seeping back into my awareness. *Oh no, please don't make me go back! Don't make me go back!* That thought screamed through my mind, and I felt desperate.

I recognized very quickly that I was now back in my old ego-consciousness state of feeling imperfect, small, fearful, and inadequate—back into the story of my life as Mary, as I identified myself with the story. What a plight! I felt exiled from my true home of God-realization, self-realization. The bliss and ecstasy were gone, and now there seemed no end to the depth of my sorrow.

I wanted to wail, but felt constrained by not wanting to call attention to myself and disturb others on the grounds. What would I say, anyway? How would I explain what had happened: "Oh, I was God-realized but I had to go back"? I was afraid they wouldn't understand, and to me, that would be even worse than keeping it to myself.

I thought, *Is this what falling from grace was all about? Is this the so-called original sin: forgetting that we're God, that we're all one with God?* I felt this was true. There is a Sanskrit word for the agony of separation, called *vipralambha,* and *agony* was indeed the only word I knew that could even begin to approach what I felt.

I wondered why I had to return to the ego state after experiencing the bliss of self-realization. The only plausible answer had to be karma—I simply had more karma that had to be lived out and experienced. I was beside myself with grief. I could barely comfort myself as I felt the torture of my own thoughts. *This is hell enough,* I thought, *feeling separate from our true nature as God/Brahman.* But even as I returned to my ego state of consciousness, I felt enormous gratitude for knowing beyond any shadow of a doubt that self-realization was the destiny of mankind—and, of particular importance to me, I knew it was my destiny as well.

In my agony of having to return to the state of ego separation, I knew I wanted more than anything to return to that state of divinity, my natural state. I wished that every person would come to experience it for at least a few moments, so they would come to know the possibility that existed within their very own being. But on this day in July 1988, I could not remain in the state of self-realization; instead, I had to return to the human consciousness of the ego-personality-mind.

A few years later, I was introduced to a poem by Hafiz, a Sufi poet, which truly spoke to my experience of the moment of being opened to self-realization:

In a Tree House

Light
Will someday split you open
Even if your life is now a cage,

For a divine seed, the crown of destiny,
Is hidden and sown on an ancient, fertile plain
You hold the title to.

Love will surely bust you wide open
Into an unfettered, blooming new galaxy

Even if your mind is now
A spoiled mule.

A life-giving radiance will come,
The Friend's gratuity will come—

O look again within yourself,
For I know you were once the elegant host
To all the marvels in creation.

From a sacred crevice in your body
A bow rises each night
And shoots your soul into God.

Behold the Beautiful Drunk Singing One
From the lunar vantage point of love.

He is conducting the affairs
Of the whole universe

While throwing wild parties
In a tree house—on a limb
In your heart.

CHAPTER 6

returning home

When I came home after the retreat, I was still reeling from my experience of self-realization. I was trying to integrate that experience with my life, which had been filled with uncertainties and unresolved issues. I tried to share with my friends the powerful transformation I'd undergone, but no one seemed able to grasp its import. This was a source of great spiritual loneliness for me, as I realized that other people couldn't understand what they had never experienced.

Over time, I discovered that what I'd gone through was not commonplace, even among those who had been on a spiritual path for years. I thought that if it had happened to me, it must have happened to others who had been on the path for much longer, but that was not the case. I wondered why I had come to self-realization relatively early in my spiritual life. When I wrote to my teacher about it, she said it was because of my faith in the spiritual energy within me. She also had someone call me three times, a week apart, to give me the message that this was a great experience. I was so grateful for these calls, as I knew with certainty that my teacher understood completely what others could not validate.

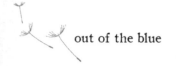

I went back to work as usual, but nothing was "as usual" inside my being. Now I knew that self-realization was the goal of this life; it was no longer a concept or something I had read and understood intellectually. For me, it was the truth. I saw that most people were too caught up in the buzz and glitz of the world to even care about getting free from it; I was caught up in the world wishing I could be free from it. I didn't mean that I wanted to leave this earth; I wished to be free on the inside, reclaiming my true nature.

Many spiritual seekers believe that once they have an experience of divine union, all their worldly problems magically disappear. That was not my experience; instead, I was unceremoniously thrown back into my life at a faster speed and with a greater ferocity to resolve my issues!

Mercifully, the experience of self-realization acted as a foundation of truth that I could hold on to. I now knew the goal of life, and I would hang on to that lifeline as I plunged once again into my existence as Mary and the painful issues yet to be resolved. There would be no running away, no easy out, no suppressing, and no pushing aside.

Trusting completely in the process of the divine path of recovery of my true nature, I continued chanting, meditating, offering service at the meditation center, and reading spiritual books. I made a conscious vow at this time to do whatever it would take to return to the state of divinity in this lifetime.

Releasing My Karmic Shackles

I felt I was living my life in a divine tornado, thrown into scenarios in all aspects of my life where I needed to apply the spiritual understandings that had been revealed to me. The wound of my mother was front and center, as the sadness of my childhood seemed to loom ever stronger. Even though I had made progress in forgiving my mother, there was still a feeling of nonacceptance when my mind would occasionally question why my childhood had to be so sad and difficult.

I also yearned to be reunited with the daughter I'd given up for adoption. I felt burdened by the traumatic memory of the day she was born: The birthing process was a painful, lonely event, as I was placed in a darkened room by myself and left by a nurse to suffer through contractions. As I screamed for help, she disdainfully told me I needed to be quiet, then left the room again. It was common back then for unwed mothers to be treated cruelly by hospital nurses, who seemed to assign themselves the job of carrying out the collective societal punishment for every young woman who became pregnant outside of marriage. At that time, unwed mothers were considered a disgrace to society and were sent away, even out of the country, to have their babies in secret, as was I.

When the doctor finally arrived to deliver my baby, he yelled at the nurse for not calling him sooner as the tearing had gone too far. I would require extensive stitches and treatment afterward to heal. Although the tissues would heal, the deep emotional wounds would remain covered over in a numbing self-reproach that stayed with me nearly all my life.

When I wanted to hold my baby, I was told this was not a good idea—I should just go home and forget it ever happened. For adoption agencies at the time, this was considered just a transaction; no counseling support was ever offered, except the suggestion that I should put it all out of my mind. That of course could never happen, and every

day I wondered and worried about my baby in silent anguish. I was too young to understand the psychological ramifications for either myself or my newborn, and the agency and medical community seemed oblivious to my inner turmoil. No one ever voiced any concern for my emotional welfare or for that of my baby.

When I returned home after leaving my newborn behind, I suffered from anxiety and spoke with a doctor to get some help. Yet instead of offering compassion and support, he accused me of turning into a neurotic and walked out of the room in disgust, telling me to take some vitamins. Today we would say that I was suffering from posttraumatic stress disorder, but that was not understood then (or at least not applied to birth mothers). No thought was given to the newborn baby, either, taken away from the mother it had come to know in utero for nine months. Society at that time was firmly against an unwed young woman keeping her baby; it simply was not tolerated. So many birth mothers back then had nervous breakdowns, developed relationship issues, or took drugs to suppress the pain of relinquishing their babies and a lifetime of societal condemnation.

I remember how awful I felt about myself following the doctor's "neurotic" pronouncement, which seemed to cement the idea that there would be no help for me in this life, as I wasn't worthy of it. A deep-seated feeling of *I am a bad person who does not deserve love* came over me. It's no wonder that I lived a life of dysfunctional relationships as the result of such profound trauma.

Many years later, I would read that birth mothers who also suffered neglect in childhood were more likely to have even worse outcomes for successful relationships in their lives, and this was very true for me. Unfulfilling relationships, along with poor choices coupled with financial struggles—these were the karmic shackles that would plague my life.

The path of recovery of my true self would eventually become the singular one of a seeker. I would need to finally take a stand and face the shame I felt inside, so it would no longer control my life. Shame is part of the ego, and it exerts much power, until you finally have the courage to face it and call it by its name. When you do, the light of truth will begin to dissolve it, as shame cannot withstand the transforming power of surrender and love.

That path of recovery would unfold a greater path of compassion for myself and others as I came to see how this path was shared by many, and my own suffering was similar to the suffering of many. But in 1988, all I knew was that if I wanted the highest state of self-realization back in this lifetime, the deep, dark corners of lack, weakness, compensation, and sorrow would need to be faced and resolved. It became clear that I was the one who had taken on this life as the journey to reclaim my true self, my divine nature— but I had no idea how difficult it would be to do so. And why was it so difficult? Because, like all human beings, I was heavily identified with the story *as* me, believing that the story *is* me.

I would need to confront the ego story I'd come into this life with and, in doing so, also resolve all the emotional issues that had kept me bound in shame and guilt.

Three Veils of Bondage

In trying to understand my own suffering, and suffering in general, I became keenly interested in the concept of *maya* and *malas* in Eastern philosophy. In my comprehension, maya is a divine power of consciousness that places

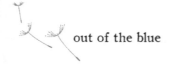

veils of duality over the mind, known as malas, which cover the experience of our true nature as God/Brahman. A veil or mala is like a cloud placed in front of the sun; the sun may be there, but we can't experience it.

There are said to be three malas: *anava mala, mayiya mala,* and *karma mala.* Anava mala is the mother of the other two malas and gives rise to feelings of unworthiness, smallness, sadness, and not being enough, as well as all kinds of insecurities. Mayiya mala gives rise to feeling separate from everyone, and dualistic comparisons that give rise to anger and envy and the sense of not belonging. Karma mala gives rise to the feeling of being the doer, as well as the feeling of limited doership, of not being able to do enough, which in turn gives rise to fear and worry.

These malas serve to create duality consciousness, which gives rise to the ego structure. The main function of ego identification is to keep us stuck in a personal story that is separate from experiencing divine union as God/Brahman. Humanity has been living for centuries as the ego-personality-mind, with stories that identify with our physical bodies and therefore the idea of mortality. Our life story lives within the concept of time in past and future, never the now.

Only God/Brahman consciousness lives in the fullness of the now, and is eternal and immortal in nature. It has no beginning or end, and lives beyond the concepts of birth and death and time. As such, it has no story, just beingness. As divine oneness consciousness descended into the human body, moving past the third eye chakra, it split into duality (maya), and the story of life as an individual— an ego separate from our divine nature—emerged.

An unconscious suffering arises when we separate from our God/Brahman nature. As I mentioned previously, there is a Sanskrit word, *vipralambha,* which describes this agony. Christians call the separation into ego "the fall from grace" and name it "sin"; but if sin exists at all, it's just the forgetfulness of our true divine nature. This is what I experienced in a profound way when I experienced self-realization, only to have to return to ego-consciousness.

Up to now, humanity has lived in a story of separateness, with each person having a separate life story of suffering that contains tragedy, grief, trauma, and feeling bad about ourselves.

Our story as an individual is always connected to ego and karma. Without ego, there would be no karma; then life would become about service from the place of divine will, which is one with all that is. As we turn inward as true seekers on the path of return, we confront the ego, resolve karma, and start toward the path of reclaiming our divine natures within. We become spiritual warriors by confronting every thought that is part of an ego story.

I really feel we need to heal in community, whether this is as few as two people or many more. We need to feel safe to tell our stories, especially the shameful and scary parts, saying how we feel and allowing ourselves to release the stuck emotions. Such moments are genuinely sacred, as that's when you release the ego story and turn to the beloved within; you feel yourself swimming in the pure waters of the divine, anointing your sacred nature as God/Brahman. Truly, it is a privilege to witness such a healing—to hear someone's story is an honor. Creating a space of unfettered love allows for healing to happen in a very organic way; then the heart unfolds like a lotus flower, releasing the jewel of divinity within.

Stepping off the "story-go-round" of the ego is part of the evolution of humanity. What will it be like when we

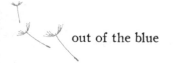

choose to step off of it, and into our true nature as God/
Brahman? I don't know exactly, as it hasn't happened yet
en masse, but most assuredly it's about bringing heaven on
earth! We'll still live in our families and communities, but
we'll do so from an awakened state, not from the ego state.

Mankind is moving from the separative, individuated,
ego state of duality and suffering, and into our true state
of God/Brahman of eternal bliss that is our true nature.
This is a journey we choose for ourselves, as no one will
drag us into self-realization. We walk this path by choos-
ing to live in our unified divine state instead of the dualistic ego-dominated one.

It is we who must battle with our own inner dragons.
This battle goes on every moment of every day, as we
make the decision to live from the responsive self rather
than the reactive ego. This is conscious living, and it takes
great inner strength. We must continue in our effort to
remember our true nature in every moment. One way to
practice this is to interrupt our mental patterns about our
story by using a mantra like *I am that I am* or whatever
phrase brings us out of our story and into remembering
our true divine, eternal nature.

We were made for great things; the royal road of self-
realization exists within for us to discover, walk, and reclaim. This union belongs to everyone as our birthright,
our divine inheritance, for as it was said:

> *Here is your divinity,*
> *the divinity that awaits all mankind.*
> *Your soul wants full expression now.*

This is the presence.
This is the living presence.
This is living. This is real.

CHAPTER 7

i experience my own death

A month after my experience of self-realization, my teenage daughter, Deborah, who up to now had been only mildly curious about meditation, consented to come with me on a weekend meditation retreat. It was an amazing experience for both of us. I watched her soul wake up to its beauty when she met my teacher. I saw the same light in my daughter's face that I'd had—it was as if someone had turned on a light switch inside her, and she woke up to the inner truth of her own divinity. She too had received a spiritual awakening.

This awakening had an amazing impact on her: At school, her grades went from C's and D's to A's and B's. On one parent night, her science teacher pulled me aside and wanted to know what had happened to Deborah. He said she was like a completely new person; she was taking responsibility in class and acting like a leader. I was delighted, and told him about the retreat she had attended.

Of course, life did continue to present challenges, but the inner door my daughter walked through opened her forever

to the truth of her divine nature. I felt so proud of all the changes she was making, and truly joyful for her.

The Teacher of My Teacher

The fall came quickly. It was now October 1988, and I was maintaining my daily practice of reading sacred texts and meditating. As I mentioned, I loved meditating outside during lunch, but when it was too cold, I'd do it on a bench in the lobby of the electrical engineering building at MIT, where I worked. It was a large lobby, with a revolving door in the middle and huge floor-to-ceiling windows on either side that faced the main street of Massachusetts Avenue.

As I sat on the bench and ate my sandwich one day, I was reading an article in a spiritual magazine recounting some experiences people had with the teacher of my teacher, who was also a self-realized monk. People talked about how they would feel so much love coming from him as he entered the room—they described his presence as a huge ocean of love washing over them, causing them to burst into tears. Another said that in the monk's presence, he could hear divine sounds inside himself, like the wind from a tornado or hurricane, or the sound of a conch shell blowing like a trumpet. I had heard of the *nada,* the divine sounds making up the universe that you can hear within your consciousness, but I hadn't experienced them personally.

I read about this monk with genuine fascination and awe, and yearned to be in his presence. I realized that this could never happen given his passing; I would have to be satisfied with reading about what it was like to meet him, instead of having that experience myself. Tears rolled down my face as I resigned myself to that thought.

I put the magazine down and closed my eyes to meditate. I sat in a relaxed cross-legged position and focused on my breath, slowly inhaling and exhaling. I could hear a few people walking through the lobby, chatting as they made their way outside through the revolving door.

After about ten minutes, I heard someone say, "Are you ready?" Thinking this was just some student walking by trying to bother me, I ignored him and kept my eyes closed. A moment passed, and again he said, "Are you ready?" This time, with my eyes still closed, I turned my attention to the voice, which came from the left of where I was sitting. I could not believe it—the monk I had been reading about was approaching! My eyes may have been closed, but I saw him as clearly as if they were open. *My God*, I thought, *I'm having one of those spiritual experiences I've heard people talk about, where they actually see someone in meditation as if in real life with their eyes open!*

The monk neared my left side, but then he turned and started moving away from me. He abruptly stopped and turned around directly in front of me. He walked straight toward me, and when he got very close, he became the swirling energy form of the Milky Way! His energy entered my solar plexus just above my navel, and I instantly began to hear many inner sounds from nature, which astounded me.

First, I heard the sound of a hurricane—it was so loud! Then I heard conches trumpeting, followed by the sound of a tornado and a locomotive. Next, I heard the ocean. Then all of the sounds blended together, along with bells ringing and the intense sound of whirling wind. I felt some of the energy go down into my legs, but the majority of it started to move up from my solar plexus and into my chest region and around my shoulders.

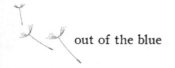

The sound got louder and louder, until it reached my eardrums. I thought, *If this continues, my eardrums will burst!* Then I realized that I was about to leave my body—to die! I wondered, *But who will take care of Deborah?* Just then, I heard a calming voice say I did not have to worry, everything would be fine. With that reassurance, I truly felt everything *would* be fine, and I let myself relax into the experience. The whole energy of my body gathered together and left through the top of my head, in a loud gust of wind.

In an instant, I traveled out of my physical body on Earth to somewhere in space. I saw two rectangular windows of light, not with the eyes of my physical body, but with my body of consciousness. Each was the size of a regular window in a house, one located directly above the other. As I gazed at these windows of light, I felt very drawn to go through them—I somehow knew that if I did, I would not return to where I had been.

The light felt like a magnetic pull of love drawing me to it. It felt so peaceful and enormously comforting; I knew this was an entrance into heaven. At that moment, the thought came again, *But what about Deborah?* The magnet of love drawing me was too strong to resist, though, and I could not help but move toward it. As I did, the monk's energy touched the left side of my energy to stop me, and he said, "Not yet."

It was not my time to enter into heaven; I had to return to where I had been. But where was that, anyway? I couldn't really remember. I wondered how I would get back, since I didn't know the way. Then I looked down, and what I saw was amazing. I saw a silver cord that looked like a filament of light about one-eighth of an inch in diameter, connected to the solar-plexus area of my light body of consciousness, just above where the navel of my physical body would be located. This cord was flexible and very, very long, extending down as far as I could see. It had a lot of slack in it and floated loosely in the air.

I understood that in order to go back to where I had been, I'd need to concentrate very hard on following the silver cord. Simultaneously, I remembered something I had read in Shirley MacLaine's book *Out on a Limb,* in which she spoke about her experience of the silver cord when she was in Peru. She had left her physical body while meditating, and saw the silver cord as she floated away from her body. As she floated higher and higher, she became frightened and immediately was back in her body. I thought, *Oh, my God, Shirley isn't crazy after all—here's the silver cord she spoke about!*

In the beginning, as I focused on following the cord, I saw only it and nothing else. It took all my strength to stay focused on it. But then, all of a sudden, the vista opened in front of me and revealed our entire solar system. I realized that wherever I was going back to was very far from where I had just been when viewing the windows of light. I could see the silver cord extending all the way in front of me, far ahead. At this point, I couldn't tell which planet I would be going to, but as I followed the cord, I realized I was going to planet Earth.

As I zipped by the other planets and got closer to Earth, I saw that I was going to North America. Zooming in, I knew I was going to the United States. Zooming in some more, I saw Massachusetts and then the town of Cambridge and then the electrical engineering building at MIT. At that point, I went through the roof of the building and was floating up by the ceiling, looking down at a body meditating on a bench, and it had the silver cord connected to it at the top of its head.

I remember thinking, *So that's the body I have to go back to.* I hadn't even known whether I would be going into a

female or a male body; that was how detached I felt from what I was viewing. I felt totally myself in this spirit state of consciousness and felt no attachment whatsoever to the physical body I was looking at on the bench. Then I followed the silver cord all the way and entered the top of the head, and finally felt my "spirit self" slip inside the physical body with a thud. When I fully entered, the body actually jumped a little. I felt as if I had entered a tight shoe. It was so confining!

At some point, I became aware of the mind and karma connected to this incarnation. *Oh no, what am I going to do? How will I ever get free of these issues, these problems?* As I immersed myself in these rather desperate thoughts, the monk's face suddenly appeared right in front of mine. I could hardly believe it. My eyes were still closed, but there he was again, as real as life. He said, "You see, the veil is very thin between here and there, very thin." Then he disappeared as quickly as he'd appeared.

A New Understanding

My God! What happened? I was sure that with this racket going on inside me, I had attracted the attention of every passerby who happened to wander through the lobby at the time. But as I opened my eyes, no one was there.

Immediately I thought, *Wow, you really can see and hear without the physical body.* As I had just experienced, you could in fact see and hear with your consciousness. When you use your senses through a physical body, you need to have your eyes and ears intact and functioning properly so the energy can work through them. Yet the actual power behind vision rests within one's consciousness.

And another, more important, thing: I had been given the experience of death! I realized that we had a big misunderstanding about what we call death—the body didn't die, because it was never alive in the first place. It just had the appearance of being alive. Therefore, there was no such thing as death! Only consciousness was alive, and it never died. The dropping away of the body was not the end of our existence, since the physical shell was a temporary puppet of the life force of consciousness. It was a housing for the light, a temple for the all-knowing, all-seeing light of consciousness. I understood that this light of consciousness contained abilities, knowledge, and wisdom all in itself, and it was not confined to time or space or to a physical body; it could travel anywhere. I wondered if that was how people were able to see things from a distance (remote viewing). I felt that was true.

For me, on that day, death itself died. Death was always a subject I feared and wondered about—but now I knew for certain that there was no such thing. You didn't die; you couldn't die, not ever! The you that is really you as consciousness cannot die. To say you live forever is quite true.

Wait a minute, I thought. *If you couldn't die and were never dead, then how could you be born? Oh, my God, birth doesn't exist, either, because how could we be born if we never died? It's all an illusion!* I realized in that moment that if there was nothing but consciousness, then when we vacate our physical body, we would pass on with the same state of consciousness. In other words, right now if we left this body, whatever state of awareness we were in would continue until we got another body in another incarnation, to develop our awareness even more. These incarnations would continue until we reached the zenith of human awareness: self-realization. Then the cycle of birth and death would no longer be necessary. The cycle of karma would be broken, and no longer would we need to live in the disunion of the ego disconnected from our divine self.

No wonder the spiritual masters urge us to wake up now and not waste this life on material pursuits. We are here to remember who we are—this is the whole point of coming here. So many thoughts and understandings whirled about in my mind as I sat there on the bench, looking out onto Massachusetts Avenue. Truly, I could not believe my good fortune in being given this most incredible experience and all the knowledge that came with it. What a great time for me! The fear of death no longer existed for me, as death itself had dissolved in the wake of my new understanding.

I realized that death is an idea born of illusion. Of course, it seemed so natural to completely identify with this physical body as myself. If I hadn't had the experience of my own divine consciousness as the real me, I could not have made the distinction. Living in a body was all so convincing that it was the only reality, along with the story that went with it. I recognized that we lived and suffered with these stories attached to an ego, rather than out of our true state of blissful divine consciousness as God/Brahman.

I also understood that even though there is no death, there is the process of letting go of the mental attachment to the physical body when it is time to leave this incarnation. I thought, *Could I make the process easier if I identified myself as my divine consciousness rather than as my physical body and its story? Could it be that my consciousness can simply leave through the top of my head as I just experienced?* I felt this was true. If it was, then it would be important for me to identify more closely with divine consciousness, to connect with my divine body of consciousness fully while still in this physical body on earth.

I thought that in the not-so-distant future, as we awakened and identified more with our divine body of consciousness, we could be more conscious participants in the so-called death process, allowing ourselves to pass out of the physical body more easily simply by being more identified as consciousness. Death, the passing out from this physical body, is something we all will experience—it is the last thing we will do on this earth, yet it seems to be the last thing we ever talk about.

I believed that meditation could be taught with the understanding that making the connection with one's divine consciousness would make passing out of the body easier by focusing on the breath, the vehicle of consciousness. I imagined if we knew for certain that we lived forever, then the fear of death would lose its grip on humanity, and how we lived each day would become more important. Then I had the realization, *There truly is no escape from bad behavior, as we live for all eternity, and where we end up after we drop the body is dependent on how we live.* This I knew for certain. I thought, *It's better to live life with the understanding that God/ Brahman lived in me as me and in everyone and to behave accordingly.* This was a sobering thought, as it meant I had to live in a very conscious way in every moment of every day and in every interaction!

I reflected on how our being here on earth was a temporary visit, and the planet and our physical bodies were like hotels. It could take many lifetimes to live out our desires and karmas, until one day our desires would begin to dry up with the dawn of self-realization.

Having had this experience of death as I sat in the lobby at MIT, I had a greater appreciation for life. I knew without any doubt that the sole purpose for taking on a body and a human birth was to experience self-realization, which was simply a part of a human's evolution. With my new understanding of death, I no longer feared it, and

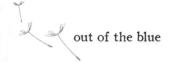

life itself took on greater significance—the importance of living fully in the moment became more real and meaningful.

I also felt intuitively that I had made a spiritual agreement to finish up all the karmas from all other lifetimes in this one, as I would not be returning to earth; I would be moving on to other spiritual realms, experiencing other states of being.

My lunchtime had stretched into an hour as all of these understandings washed over me, one after another. This great experience of death felt so simple; my consciousness just went out the top of my head like smoke going up a chimney. I remembered reading somewhere that a yogi could experience his own death while still alive. I had always wondered what that meant and how that would be possible. Now I knew for myself!

I went back to my office feeling completely changed inside. I could hardly wait to talk to some of my friends, who were also on the same spiritual path, about what happened. I wondered if they'd had this experience in their meditations, too, but had never felt comfortable sharing it.

As I shared my amazing experience of death, I discovered, much to my disappointment, that no one else had had this experience. I realized it was time to once again immerse myself in the practices of meditation, service, and contemplation rather than trying to share these experiences—perhaps that would come at another time. For now, I knew I still had much to resolve in myself. And I had the sense that much more was to come. I continued on with my life, trying to incorporate all the lessons.

CHAPTER 8

three meetings

It was now 1990. My daughter and I traveled to see my mother in New Jersey about once a month, staying for the weekend.

One day we were having lunch, and I said, "Hey, Mom, would you like to do something different this summer?" She replied, "Sure, I was feeling like I'd like to try something different." When I asked if she'd like to come with her granddaughter and me to meet the monk we had been talking about for the last few years, she said, "Yes."

Mother Meets the Monk

Finally the day came. I had been at the retreat site with Deborah for the past week, and she stayed there while I went to pick up my mother. When she and I arrived back at the retreat, we met my daughter at the front door as planned. Deborah greeted us with the message that the monk would be meeting the three of us together! I was amazed, as it was unusual to have personal meetings apart from the crowd.

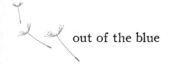

As we waited on a bench among hundreds of people, I marveled at my mother's great fortune at having a private meeting with the self-realized monk as her first introduction. I thought that perhaps I had underestimated my mother.

When it was our turn to see my teacher, the three of us walked forward, arms entwined, with my mother in between my daughter and myself. The monk said, "Three generations." I thought it was such an amazing blessing to have three generations in the company of an enlightened one who could awaken innate divinity and provide spiritual guidance.

As we grew closer, my mother leaned over and handed the monk something. *What could that be?* I wondered. *I didn't even see her carrying anything. How strange.* With great joy, the monk said, "For me?" My mother answered with a simple "Yes." She'd handed a beautiful hand-sewn heart-shaped pillow made out of white silk to the monk, who in turn pulled my mother toward her. My teacher embraced her with great love, saying, "Grandmother!" I stood in awe over the entire sight. My mother was being received with the same pure respect and love she'd so clearly shown the monk.

My mother was soon offered a chair, while Deborah and I sat on the floor in front of the monk. It had been raining very heavily, like a monsoon, and my teacher told my mother, "You brought the rain." By then, I had begun to really question my opinion of my mother, as rain is considered a sign of great blessings, and evidently her presence was being acknowledged as one who'd brought blessings.

This had a profound effect on me, and I felt a shift inside myself regarding my mother. I could feel a subtle emotional wall, which had always been there after she'd left the family when I was so young, begin to soften. It was apparent that a deep healing was being bestowed upon our family . . . and that wasn't the end of it.

All of a sudden, my teacher leaned forward, looking right into my eyes, and asked if I had another daughter. *Why is she bringing this up now?* I wondered. I knew she was aware that I had two daughters—Deborah, whom I had raised and was now sitting by my side, and the one I had given up for adoption over 25 years ago—because I had written to her about both of them in the past. Her words penetrated and reverberated in my being; I was so astonished that I was unable to speak.

Deborah answered, "There's only me." My mind kept repeating the words, *I have two, I have two,* but my mouth could not speak them. Then the conversation shifted as the monk sat back in her chair, and the meeting went on for about another 15 minutes. We were then ushered out of the room with a gift of a box of chocolates.

After the meeting, I became obsessed with thinking about the daughter I had given up for adoption. *What does it mean that my teacher had brought up the subject? Will my child and I be reunited soon? I hope so.* I decided that I would ask the monk about my adopted daughter at the public program to be held in a few days.

When the time came to see the monk for a few moments, I asked her about my daughter. She put up her hand, as in a blessing, and I knew that everything would be all right and I would be reunited with my daughter someday. I'd had only a glimpse of my baby after giving birth to her, and I so wanted to finally hold her now.

After the retreat, my relationships with my mother and with Deborah improved, as we became more open-hearted with each other. I also tied up loose ends with old friendships, so I could move on in my life.

A Meeting with Jesus

Shortly after returning home from the retreat, I had a very powerful dream that clarified my relationship with the monk. I was in a heavenly place with a soft bluish light spreading out everywhere, yet there was no sun and no moon. I looked out onto a completely flat terrain, and wondered where the light was coming from. There were hundreds of people seated three feet apart on the ground in meditation, wrapped in white shawls and robes. They were completely still, and the silence was palpable. All of a sudden a man with a long white beard, who was also wrapped in a white shawl, stood up. I knew I was to be offered a place to meditate. As I had that thought, the man gestured for me to sit down.

As I started to sit, a laserlike beam of white light appeared, aimed at my heart. I followed the light beam to its source—there in front of me was a ten-foot square platform about six inches in height. In the middle of the platform, seated in the lotus posture on a chair, was Jesus! He was surrounded by a few people who were also seated, but directly on the platform itself. Everyone was in the white shawls and robes, as was Jesus. His eyes were blue, his skin olive; his full beard and long hair were brown in color.

I knelt down in front of him and felt very upset, wondering where he'd been all this time. I had missed him so much, and was heartbroken that he'd left me. With angry tears in my eyes and pain in my heart, I said, "You promised me fulfillment."

He looked deeply into my eyes, and I felt his compassionate love enter my heart. My anger melted into a profound love for him, and I felt myself merging with his divine energy. Just then his face began to disappear, and in its place was the face of the monk. I immediately understood that my teacher was here to complete the promise of fulfillment Jesus had made to me so many years ago.

When I awoke, I was amazed. The dream felt completely real, and I knew beyond any shadow of a doubt that I had actually met Jesus in the spiritual realm. His love felt like a soothing balm. I also felt so grateful to be in the company of my teacher, to complete my spiritual journey on earth through self-realization.

Meeting with the Devil

In the fall of 1991, I had a most astonishing and powerful dream in which I met the devil. Now, I should say that I really don't believe in the devil as a separate entity who is doing something to me. Instead, the energy of the devil is more like part of the ego structure we identify with that convinces us we are small, not of any value, and separate from God, our divine nature. Earlier in the book, I mentioned *mayiya mala,* which is the same idea; the term refers to a small part of consciousness veiling our divine nature, making us feel separate and unworthy. That sure sounds like the devil to me. Perhaps we should call this small part of consciousness the "ego-devil."

In the dream, I was in a place that was so dark all around, it was like standing in a black void. I couldn't define the place as having any walls, and there was gray smoke rising from the ground. Someone was walking toward me through the smoke: It was a man dressed in a dark suit, shirt, and tie, and he was carrying a briefcase. His hair was dark and slicked back, he had a widow's peak hairline, and his skin color was gray. I had the thought, *This is the devil!* He looked at me, and I looked at him. Neither of us spoke. I

felt no fear; I was just rather amused that the devil looked like the typical caricature we have all seen in movies or pictures. This truly was a meeting with an archetype.

Some say the devil archetype represents our "shadow side," also known as the ego-consciousness, concerning attachments—dwelling on things that bring possessive pleasure and aversions, such as people or things that we dislike and the seven deadly sins. One way we can help release this shadow side is to remember our divine nature as our true identity. Forgetfulness of our divine nature makes us suffer in ego separation. Some ways we can foster remembering our true identity is to meditate every day, even for a few minutes; read from a sacred text before going to sleep; or keep the company of others who are on a spiritual path. There are numerous ways to stay in remembrance of our divine nature.

In the dream, there was a wooden bench to my left, and the devil sat down upon it without saying a word. I sat next to him, and he put the briefcase on his lap and snapped open the two latches. He took out a book and opened to a page. I had the impression it was the Akashic Records, said to be a consciousness database of every thought, word, or deed recorded energetically in a soul's life.

He turned to me and matter-of-factly said, "I can't have anything to do with you anymore, as you have chosen the path of love." I was given to understand that I needed to sign the book, which I did. He signed as well. I further understood that with this signing, my relationship with the devil was forever severed. No other words were exchanged.

He placed the book back in his briefcase, closed it, and got up from the bench. As he walked away from me back into the dark gray smoke, to my surprise, he turned,

smiled, and gave a final wave good-bye, as if to say, "No hard feelings." I waved back, and he disappeared for good into the dark smoke.

When I awoke, I felt very happy. I knew I had completed enough inner work to help free myself from this devil archetype within my consciousness. This buoyed my spirit, as I knew it was another important milestone on the path to recover my true state of divinity. I also knew that I needed to keep going, to keep to my daily practices and continue confronting emotional roadblocks along the way.

This meeting with the devil bolstered my confidence, as I knew for certain, deep inside my heart, that I was innately a good person. For as the devil himself had said, I had chosen the path of love; I had chosen my divine nature over ego-devil identification.

CHAPTER 9

creation and
the void

In the summer of 1992, I found myself at a kind of spiritual standstill, when some friends signed up for a self-improvement course and invited me to attend. The course was described as an intense four-day event, from 8 A.M. to 9 P.M., focusing on uncovering and clearing away recurring mental and emotional patterns that kept a person stuck in their life. I figured it would be great to be in an environment with a group of people all focused on the same desire to release old patterns. There was no spiritual content to the course, but rather a philosophical one in how to live one's life more fully.

When I first signed up for the workshop, I inwardly asked for my teacher's blessings so that whatever needed to be revealed would be, and I could live in union with my divine nature of God/Brahman. Having invoked grace, I went to my first class.

These classes proved to be very demanding. Sometimes we would share in pairs; sometimes in groups of ten; and then with the entire group, which consisted of about 200

people. On the afternoon of the last day, we were all gathered in a room and the entire group was sharing together. One woman spoke about her experience of being physically assaulted. Even though it had happened many years ago, she was clearly still in great pain and struggling to process this event.

The instructor talked about looking at this event from a different, more detached point of view. She said that we usually come from a perspective of seeing some event as either good or bad. "But," she asked, "what if you looked at an event as neither inherently good nor bad, but just as an event?" The woman, of course, balked at this thought, as I would have, had it happened to me.

The instructor pressed on: "You know, some people might say that this event wasn't bad; some might say it was good, at least from the standpoint that it started you looking at your whole life differently. You say that you developed more compassion for others after it happened. Therefore, some might say that what happened was good—while you feel, and others might say, that what happened was bad. Do you see what I'm saying? An event happened, and someone labeled it bad while someone else labeled it good. But perhaps it was neither good nor bad; perhaps it could be looked at as just an event."

A man in the group stood up and said, "It sounds like you're talking about the void." He went on to say that the spiritual void is a state of nothingness, just a neutral state of being.

Up until now, I was sitting in my chair listening to this very interesting philosophical discussion, but then something remarkable happened: when he said the word *void*, I was given an experience of the void!

As I sat in my chair, I felt a bolt of lightning, shooting from the heavens above, go right through the top of my head, all the way down my spine. My whole consciousness was thrown into the void—I was suddenly in a very deep, black, velvety outer space. Although all I saw was black, the void wasn't empty. Rather, it had a presence in it that emanated deep, silent love. It was the God source.

Just then I saw the huge mouth of God, which spanned the heavens. God's mouth was wide open, and out of it spilled all kinds of forms: vegetables, trees, plants, animals, and on and on. It reminded me of a gigantic cornucopia! At the same time, I heard the sound of *Om (Aum)*. It was a constant sound, recurring over and over again in the background, like a drone. I had an immediate understanding that this sound was going on all the time, all around me everywhere, and it had no beginning and it had no end— the *nada*.

I knew that *Om* was the sound of God, and the feeling associated with God was divine love. Even though the sound was constantly occurring, we typically don't hear it. I had read that some hear the nada in meditation, just as I was hearing it now, and had heard it while meditating on the bench at MIT. I also felt God as an eternal emanating energy of divine love—the sound of *Om* was this divine love, and it pulsed all around me and in me.

The whole world had been created from this *Om* and was being continually transformed, maintained, and destroyed and re-created again in an endless cycle. This meant that every moment was being re-created, and nothing stayed the same. All the galaxies were suspended and held in place by this vibrational force of God. It was like a divine glue; everything floated in and was held together by this constant *Om,* including us! I understood that since we are God, our vibrational consciousness was also made of *Om.* Everything, including us, is consciousness —and consciousness is light, and light is a wave vibration,

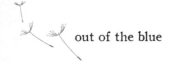

and every wave vibration has a sound, and that sound is *Om*. Sound, light, and love are all wave vibrations of energy, and this is what our divine consciousness is made from: *Om*.

If we are *Om*, then we too create using *Om*. I thought about our creative process: First we have the desire for something, then we think about creating it, then we talk about creating it, and then we actually make it appear. All of this comes from a thought vibration called an "idea." We open our mouths like God, and out comes the blueprint for a creation from an idea. Of course, the process takes a little longer here on earth, since most of us are not in perfect union with our Godness; but if we were, things would happen almost instantly.

Some speak of the void as nothing, but I experienced it as the *no-thing*. It wasn't nothing; it was something. It was the pure, divine, unfettered, loving presence of God.

The experience and understanding of the void all seemed to happen in a split second. When my consciousness reentered my body and went back to normal, I jumped up from my chair, threw my hands up in the air, and shouted, "I've got it!"

As I exclaimed those words, I felt so much love emanating from me—in particular, from my third-eye chakra. I could feel a beacon of light pouring from between my eyes, much like a miner's light on a helmet. I felt ablaze with love and very peaceful.

The teacher asked, "What have you got?"

I couldn't believe I had jumped up like that—that wasn't like me. What was I going to say? I stammered out something like, "Love . . . there is only love all around. The *no-thing* is not nothing, it is love." I hesitated to say

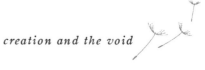

the word *God,* replacing it instead with the word *love.* My revelation was greeted with silence, as people looked at me rather quizzically. I sat down, and the teacher continued with her dialogue.

Shortly afterward, the class took a break. As I waited in line in the ladies' bathroom, I still felt the love suffusing my entire being. When I looked at myself in the mirror, I could see light coming from my head and face. I was quite amazed by this and felt very fortunate to be in this state.

Someone next to me mentioned that I looked different, and another ventured to ask what had happened to me. "Oh," I said, "I experienced that all there is is love, all around, nothing but love." I didn't quite know what else to say, and it seemed neither did they. I was happy when the class officially ended that day so I could be by myself in this state of love and contentment.

At home, since I was living alone, I could revel in this state of peace and love uninterrupted. My mind was so quiet and still; it wasn't thinking its usual self-deprecating thoughts, which seemed to have a life of their own and played like background music. Instead, I was in a state of being free and having hardly *any* thoughts, a state of happiness.

As I sat in my kitchen, I had the experience of my mind as a black box, hovering next to my head. It was a construct of energy in which I could have thoughts and use them as needed to manage information useful in interacting with the world. I didn't have to have any thoughts at all if I didn't want to—in that case, I would just be in my natural state of blissful being and contentment. Most of my life had been spent being the victim of my own mind, unable to control the thoughts constantly flowing through it, mostly with self-doubt and self-deprecation.

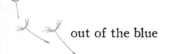

Now I understood with great clarity that this was the state of most of mankind.

I remembered reading the advice from sages that says you should have one less thought a day until you have no thoughts at all, so it must be possible. I was experiencing something very close to that state, and I liked it a whole lot.

When I looked in the mirror, the light continued to pour from my forehead. I relished this state, hoping it would last forever. Although it didn't, I did get to live in it for 24 hours and was given a glimpse again into the divine state of consciousness that lived inside.

When I returned to my normal state, the many thoughts of self-deprecation and self-doubt returned. I wasn't dismayed by this, however, as I knew that one day, when the time was right, I would return to my natural state of divine consciousness. One day, I would be free of the self-deprecating state of the ego-personality-mind.

CHAPTER 10

the reunion

In 1994, my father passed. A few months before this, I had sent him a letter that expressed all the love and appreciation I had for him, and I was so glad I'd had the time to see him at Christmas before he left his body. A month after he passed he came to me in a dream to let me know that he was doing well, and he seemed very happy.

My father had left me a little inheritance, which made it possible for me to take a trip to India to see my teacher and immerse myself in spiritual study. A few months after my return, I got a phone call from a social worker. As soon as she announced who she was, I knew that the call was about my daughter, the one I'd given up for adoption. The social worker wanted to know if I wanted to talk with her, and I immediately said yes. A stream of questions came pouring out of me: "How is she? What's her name? Where does she live? Is she okay?" I had named my daughter Margaret, but the social worker told me that her adoptive parents had named her Cyndi and she lived in New Jersey.

After I hung up with the social worker, the phone rang again. When I answered, I heard my daughter's voice for the first time. "Hello, Mary?"

"Yes."

"Mom?"

"Yes!"

She started crying, and I was amazed that her voice sounded so much like mine. We made plans for a reunion in a month.

When I got off the phone, I was in a state of emotional numbness. It took me a few days to figure out that this numbness was covering over all the feelings I had about leaving my daughter behind when she was born. I found a support group who worked with reunions of this kind, which gave me an opportunity to work through some of the profound heartbreak and lack of self-worth I felt surrounding the relinquishment of my baby.

Even so, the day I was to see Cyndi, I felt a deep grief well up inside. It was so intense that I fell to my knees in sorrow and began to weep. I thought, *How am I ever going to be able to process all this? How am I ever going to forgive myself?* I felt terrible about walking away from my baby, although I'd had no real choice at the time.

I needed to pull myself together if I was going to be able to drive the four hours to our reunion. I called out, "Please, God, help me!" Just then, the phone rang, and I was surprised to find a very dear friend of mine, Aditi, on the other end. She asked, "Mary, how are you?" After catching my breath, I told her what was going on and how I'd called out to God for help.

"That's why I'm calling!"

"What?" I said in disbelief.

"Last night I was awakened at two in the morning with a poem writing itself in my mind, and I could not go back to sleep until I wrote it down," she told me. "It's about you and Cyndi—I knew you would be leaving soon to see her. I didn't know it was today, but I knew I had to call you right away and read the poem to you. I know it was from God. He wants you to understand that what happened had to happen, and you mustn't blame yourself. There are reasons for things . . . but you know that. I'll read the poem to you now, since I think it will help. When you get back, I'll give you a copy."

I said I could hardly believe she was calling me with a poem at the exact moment I'd pleaded for help. Here is what she read:

Soul's Journey

Blessed is the mother earth
Great fortune has dawned upon her
The sun smiles gently and bursts brilliantly
over the mighty oceans, the roaring rivers,
the peaceful lakes, the flowing creeks,
and the gentle ponds.
The emerald world is blanketed in light that greets us
with all the treasures it holds,
like a baby in mother's arms,
The carpeted dunes sing out in joy
rippling sand in rhythm,
Rocky mountains loom in awe
shocking, alluring, mysterious,
Flowers bloom in rainbow colors,
swaying in the wind with ecstasy,
Fragrant, meditative memory of God,
Singing, dancing, leaping joyfully,
the Universe is immersed in Grace.
A soul is born
to reach for enlightenment
aiming at the truth,
Drenched in the nectar of life

with a taste for pain and pleasure alike,
Go above and beyond
and merge with the divine.

I made it to New Jersey—finally, after 30 years, I was going to hold my daughter in my arms. As she walked through the door, Cyndi said, "Mom?" I just said, "It's me." We fell into each other's arms and sobbed for several minutes, unable to speak. She told me that she had always felt me with her on a spiritual level and had always loved me. We were deeply connected, and reunited as mother and daughter.

This reunion healed places in me I didn't even know needed healing. My family completely accepted Cyndi as one of their own, but the same was not true for me with Cyndi's adopted family or her husband. They saw me as an unwelcome intruder, someone who would upset the family balance. I also felt their cultural judgment reserved for unwed mothers who relinquished their babies, just like the nurses at the hospital where I'd given birth. This was a source of great emotional pain for Cyndi and me; because of that, we would rarely see each other after the reunion, although we stayed in touch. To this day, this healing continues for both of us.

With all that needed to happen in the years following my experience of self-realization, it wasn't any wonder that I could not have remained in that state back in July 1988; so much needed to be revealed, resolved, and healed, and these were not little things. Karma is such a mystery in the way it needs to be worked out—no wonder the spiritual masters have asked us to have compassion for ourselves and others.

CHAPTER 11

a seismic shift in understanding true healing

Some years passed, and I continued on with work, life with my family and friends, and my spiritual studies. I often visited the meditation retreat site where my teacher resided, as well as a meditation center near my home.

It was now the winter of 1999. I wasn't feeling well and was diagnosed with Hashimoto's thyroiditis, an auto-immune disease where the body produces antibodies against the thyroid. In other words, my own immune system was attacking my thyroid gland, which regulates metabolism. I was told that the condition was incurable and I'd need to take drugs for the rest of my life. I started taking medication right away as my thyroid was in very bad shape, and I felt awful. After researching some other choices, I switched to a natural supplement that worked far better. Still, I wanted to understand the cause of the thyroiditis.

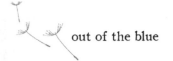

Since I knew that emotions play a primary role in our illnesses, I prayed to the powers that be to help me understand the reason behind my failing thyroid, and to find a practitioner who knew a method to cure it. The next day I mentioned this to a colleague at work who said, "You're going to need homeopathy," and thrust a flyer into my hand that read, "Homeopathy, the gentle mind/body medicine."

I reflected on how many times I had seen those little tubes of over-the-counter homeopathic remedies in stores, but never quite knew what to do with them because I didn't know what they were for or how they worked. I was also captivated by the words *gentle mind/body medicine.* Trusting that this was the answer to my prayer, and recognizing the divine principle of synchronicity at work, I immediately made an appointment with the practitioner in the flyer, who was a fellow registered nurse.

A Deeper Understanding of Myself
Through Homeopathy

I filled out the forms the practitioner sent, and was amused by the question, "What do your friends complain about when interacting with you?" I chuckled to myself in a self-revealing way when I thought of the answer: *They think I'm a know-it-all!*

Another question asked if I had any recurring dreams, which I did. For the greater part of my adult years, I dreamed I was standing on the beach, watching a gigantic wave coming toward me that was as huge as a ten-story building. I stood there, terrified, knowing I could not escape it as it came over me—then the dream ended.

I was also asked to fill out a timeline of "never well since" (NWS) events in my life. These referred to any physical or emotional trauma or life event that had left a lasting impact and altered my mental, emotional, or physical body in some way from that point onward. Examples of some people's NWS events might be: "I was never well since my dog died; I still haven't gotten over it," "I was never well since I had that car accident; I still have nightmares," or "I was never well since I had that injection [or took that drug]."

Clearly, this homeopathic consultation was a very individualized approach aimed at who I was versus what disease I had. Looking at the timeline in front of me, I saw a lifetime of NWS events of grief and loss regarding relationships. No wonder my thyroid was failing; the throat is a place of expression and unexpressed grief, and conversations were still stuffed deep inside me.

Of course, the usual family history question was asked: "What did your parents suffer from concerning their health?" The NWS timeline actually began with any ill effects my mother might have suffered when she was pregnant with me—in homeopathy, the timeline of our life starts with the emotional and physical state of the mother even before conception, and certainly during pregnancy. I had to call my mother to find out what her pregnancy was like for her, and if she had suffered any emotional, physical, or environmental adversities.

I was stunned when she said, "Oh, yes, when I was eight months pregnant with you, my mother died."

When I asked what impact this had had on her, she replied, "It was terrible. My mother was my best friend, and I never got over it. After you were born, we had to have relatives come and take care of you as I could hardly function."

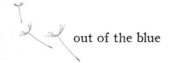

There it was: the foundation for grief and loss over *mother* set in utero, imprinting my psyche! The foundation of bonding in relationships had also been set, as my mother could neither bond with me emotionally nor nurture me because she was in too much grief over the loss of *her* beloved mother. In our conversation, she also revealed that when she was 19, she'd had to give up her own baby for adoption, as she wasn't married at the time! My mother had carried that secret and deep grief and shame long before she became pregnant with me. And it was amazing how the same event had happened to me when I was 19.

When I got off the phone, I cried for her and I cried for me.

The Laws of Homeopathy

Just a note here before I go any further: If you choose to use homeopathy, I ask that you work with a qualified practitioner of your choice and not treat yourself. Many things need to be considered, and only a trained practitioner can effectively assist in these matters. There are medical doctors, registered nurses, and other health-care practitioners with a homeopathic practice you can consult; you can go to the website of the National Center for Homeopathy to locate a homeopath (www.homeopathycenter.org) or ask your friends to refer someone.

I went to my first appointment with a feeling of curiosity and hopefulness that somehow this gentle mind/body medicine could help with all the layered grief of my life and support my thyroid to heal. The homeopathic interview consisted mainly of me talking about issues in my life and how I felt about them. I asked a lot of questions about how the practice worked and was fascinated by the answers.

First I learned that the basic law of homeopathy is "like cures like," nature's law of healing, which also applies to us since we are a part of nature. This law was known to Hippocrates, the father of medicine, as "the law of similars." But it was Samuel Hahnemann, M.D., a German physician and chemist who proved its real value by rediscovering the law and developing the homeopathic method of preparation of substances, as well as the homeopathic system based on its law of cure.

This basic law of similars means that any substance that could cause symptoms in a healthy person can heal anyone experiencing the same symptoms. Thus, micro doses of the substance are prepared through a scientific process that dilutes the substance so no material particles are present, just the energetic information, and these small substances stimulate the body's own innate vital healing force. (Homeopathy is an entirely different system from herbal medicine, as herbology uses material rather than energetic doses.)

Hahnemann believed there was no such thing as disease but rather disharmony in the "vital force," another name for the living consciousness of the body, which runs all the functions of the physical body as well as the mind and emotions. He understood that the primary connection between the mind and body must be addressed and brought to harmony for a cure to occur and physical symptoms to resolve. He said that symptoms are important because they provide an evidentiary road map (symptom picture) to the correct selection of a matching remedy.

Homeopathic remedies are made from nature: plants, minerals, and animal substances. Hahnemann and his fellow doctors tested these remedies on themselves before giving them to the sick, using a scientific technique called a

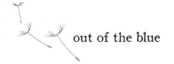

"proving": To find the curative value of each substance, the substance would be prepared in homeopathic doses and given in overdose amounts to 50 healthy people, known as "provers." These people would then observe and report the mental, emotional, and physical changes they experienced. When the provers stopped taking the remedy, their symptoms would disappear over time. These symptoms would be catalogued in a book called a "homeopathic repertory" and each remedy and its symptom picture would be written into a materia medica.

Today, homeopaths have software programs with the repertory and materia medica to make it easier to find the right remedy. I foresee a time when a user-friendly version will be available to the public as we become more knowledgeable about this system, thus creating a healer in every household.

After my almost two-hour appointment, I left with my remedy bottle (a bottle of water with the remedy in it) to take the first dose at home. The practitioner also loaned me a book, *Portraits of Homoeopathic Medicines, Volume 1: Psychophysical Analyses of Selected Constitutional Types,* by Catherine R. Coulter, as I wanted to read about the remedy she suggested. As a fellow RN, she'd seen my fascination with this new (at least to me) system of medicine. This book appealed to me because I always had an interest in psychology—as it turned out, homeopathy would satisfy that intellectual pursuit on every level!

Although the remedy the practitioner had suggested was not my homeopathic constitutional type—that is, it didn't match my innate personality on the mental/emotional/physical level that I was born with—it did fit the layer of grief, lack of nurturance, and mourning of a

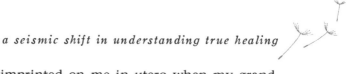

dead mother imprinted on me in utero when my grand-mother had died. The proving of this remedy, whose main delusion or fixed idea is *the mother is dead,* meaning that the mother is either literally dead or emotionally unavailable, fit my story perfectly . . . including the recurring dream of being overcome by the ocean.

After the long consultation with the practitioner, I was told that my NWS timeline, including my physical symptoms and sharing my story, matched the remedy *Natrum muriaticum,* which is ordinary table salt but pre-pared homeopathically in a high dilution to unlock the healing power of that mineral.

An extraordinary thing happened when I first took Natrum muriaticum. It caused a seismic shift in all I pre-viously thought I'd known about disease, germs, cure, pre-vention, healing, and mind/body medicine in a way I could never have imagined.

So __This__ Is How It Works!

I was standing at the sink in my kitchen, holding my remedy bottle: a red plastic bottle filled with water and the colorless, odorless, highly diluted homeopathic remedy Natrum muriaticum. I opened the bottle, pouring one tea-spoon of the remedy into a four-ounce cup of water, stirring vigorously; then I placed one teaspoon from the cup into my mouth, discarding the rest of the water into a nearby plant.

As I placed the teaspoon of remedy into my mouth, my whole consciousness flew out into the deep, dark cos-mos. In this space I saw the part of my consciousness where my mind/emotions had been stuck for so many years: it was the grief over my mother I had carried all these years,

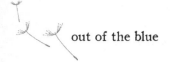

imprinted in utero and then repeated throughout my life in my closest relationships. The area of stuck hurt twinkled like a star, and then I saw the consciousness of the remedy coming from the right to greet it, twinkling in the same way. As the two twinkling stars met each other, they seemed to dissolve together, and I felt a release of energy in my mind. With this release, my awareness instantly went back into my body.

I had an immediate understanding that this remedy was alive, knowing where my mind/emotions were stuck. Amazed, I shouted out loud, "So *this* is how it works; it works on the level of consciousness!" I'd clearly just been given the experience of the law of similars—the living consciousness of a human is healed with the living consciousness of nature through this innate law.

My mind reeled with the importance of this experiential knowledge. I thought, *So disease begins in consciousness, and it gets healed in consciousness as well.* I remembered what Jesus had said to me 13 years earlier: "Now do you understand what disease is all about?" At that time, he'd given me the understanding that all disease in the physical body begins first on an energetic level in emotions and thoughts; in other words, on the level of consciousness.

It was clear that thoughts and emotions can *affect* the brain and the rest of the physical body, but they are not generated *from* the brain. They exist independently in our consciousness, which surrounds and innervates the body. Anxiety, depression, grief, fear, and all mental suffering must be addressed from the consciousness—I was now being given the experience that this is the territory for the gentle mind/body consciousness–based medicine of homeopathy.

I saw and felt the remedy as a living divine force. I remembered once reading about plants, flowers, and minerals as living *devas* and *devis,* Sanskrit words meaning feminine and masculine divine forces. I realized, *This remedy is a living force of the divine! Nature is truly God's medicine basket, governed by divine laws of healing.* I knew I had to study this amazing system of medicine, not only for my sake but for the sake of my family. And I at once understood the impact for all of humanity.

As my consciousness returned to normal, I took the red plastic bottle with the precious remedy and bowed inwardly to the divine living substance of Natrum muriaticum. I sat down and began to read about it from the book loaned to me by the practitioner, and was spellbound by the accuracy of the description of the state of mind of Natrum muriaticum. In fact, it was such an accurate description of my inner state that I laughed out loud.

I thought, *How can my inner state be known so perfectly? I thought it was unique to me. Wait! I see now that the inner state is just a state of mind, clearly not personal only to me, and can be changed; it's not a life sentence! Aha! So homeopathy can help clear the troubled, traumatized minds of humanity to prevent disease in our biological bodies—hence, it's the perfect mind/body medicine! Not only that, there is a remedy for nearly every state of mind.*

I sat for hours reading the 58-page description of Natrum muriaticum with a profound respect for table salt and Mother Nature. As I read, I felt an old sad memory come up suddenly, and I burst out crying. After the tears subsided, I felt so much better. Another half hour passed, then the same thing happened with another memory. I realized that this was the remedy at work, unearthing stuck consciousness in the form of feelings and memories, and bringing them up and out. There was a quality to this experience that was not just a rehash of emotions; it felt like a clearing, a true healing. Every time a release happened, I

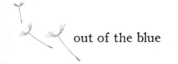

felt a wonderful sense of well-being. Later I learned that this was to be expected when the right remedy has been chosen.

People often have what is known as a "remedy dream," and receiving one is a way to know that the correct remedy is being taken. You'll know you're having one because it has a different feeling to it than an ordinary dream, and addresses an issue you're struggling to resolve.

That night, I had such a dream: A generic person representing my relationship issues approached me, and we settled our differences and walked away peacefully. I slept very deeply and awoke refreshed and happy.

The next night, I dreamed I was near a big body of water, but this time it did not overpower me. I realized that water was the symbol for emotions, and now I was able to release my feelings of grief instead of being drowned by them. Now I could begin to successfully navigate and then release my emotions.

I remained on this remedy for many months with the guidance of my practitioner, taking it as needed according to my mental/emotional state. Physical symptoms abated, my energy level improved, and I was able to cut down on my natural thyroid remedy. I felt happier inside and a little stronger emotionally.

Over days, months, and years, the sadness from my childhood melted away, and I felt a happier inner life.

Never again would I unconsciously suffer from the grief and fixed idea of *the mother is dead*. No longer would I look outside myself to *get* love; now I *became* love from within myself, and could share it without the focus of trying to get it from someone else. I felt free from the mental reruns

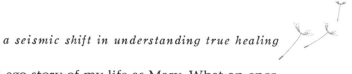

of the hurtful ego story of my life as Mary. What an enormous relief!

I understood that the bond between me and my mother hadn't been created in a healthy way because she was unable to be emotionally available when I was young. After taking Natrum muriaticum, the sense of rejection vanished. I was able to open to the divine love that had always been around me but could not be let in before; I was able to find the love in my own heart that had always been available. Of course, sometimes traces of that old grief surfaced, but I was no longer stuck in it in an unconscious way. I had the tools now to acknowledge these traces and then let them pass through.

The Necessity of Consciousness-Based Systems

I discovered that if we were free of the inner dialogue of our stories, completely free, then the only story present would be the eternal experience of bliss as God/Brahman beings—our true selves fulfilling our true destiny, creating a heaven on earth for each other. I know that as we evolve into self-realized beings, all areas that serve humanity must naturally evolve as an organic response, including our medical, educational, financial, environmental, and social systems.

For me, homeopathy is the natural evolutionary response in our medical system, as we come to know consciousness as the basis of life itself. I could see the importance of this consciousness-based system assisting humanity in evolving from being stuck in the idea of disease and the ego story of unhappiness to reclaiming our inheritance as divine beings living happier, healthier lives. Indeed, if we are to become masters of our lives, we must

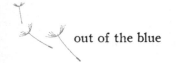

master every aspect of ourselves, including our health. We must remember how to heal ourselves.

Since we are in fact multidimensional (mental/emotional/spiritual/physical) rather than one-dimensional (physical) beings, we must have a *whole* system of medicine, a multidimensional system. Consciousness-based medicine (homeopathy) provides a balanced system, treating the whole person in every instance; homeopathic medicine and allopathic trauma-based medicine, in union, would provide that wholeness.

I felt an urgent need to study homeopathy. I simply *had* to study it; it felt like a calling. Right then and there, I decided to go back to school at the age of 55. I wondered if I would be up to the rigors of becoming a student again, but any doubts were simply washed away by the excitement of the intellectual and spiritual adventure. Homeopathy would bridge the gap for me between science, nature, and the divine, proving consciousness as the primary living vital force of healing, of life itself—a living, intelligent force with principles, rules, and regulations, alive with love and bliss and healing.

CHAPTER 12

back to school

I told my practitioner that I needed to go back to school and study this amazing system of medicine. She said I was in luck, because one of the foremost homeopathic physicians and scholars would soon be coming to Boston to teach for the next three years. I knew this was divine serendipity at work, and I completely embraced it.

Sitting for so many hours in classrooms at my age was difficult; in fact, it was downright painful! But I was so riveted by the information I was receiving from this neurologist turned homeopathic physician that it far outweighed the physical discomfort.

In studying homeopathy, I did not abandon my training as a registered nurse or my respect for allopathy; rather, I was expanding my training to include consciousness as the living principle governing the biological physical body. What homeopathy gave me was the understanding of the life principle *behind* the physical body—that of living consciousness—and a medical system of working with this consciousness to prevent and cure disease by fostering harmony in the mind/emotions according to the innate law of healing, the law of similars.

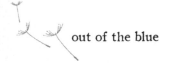

Returning homeopathic medicine to our health-care system would be ideal, expanding our current system that primarily focuses on the physical, material level to include the homeopathic consciousness-based system to address the mind/body connection. It would also be far more cost-effective if the general public were taught basic courses in preventive and acute homeopathic home care for minor issues, using affordable remedies that are proven to work well and without side effects. There is nothing greater than knowing how to help yourself and your family with every-day acute health issues; this would have the added benefit of freeing up emergency rooms for true emergencies.

To this day, this system of medicine has continued to amaze me with its complexity, elegance, and proven effectiveness in the prevention and cure of so many epidemics, as well as acute and chronic disease. Its affordability, gentleness, absence of toxic effects, and general availability make it truly the medicine of the people!

The History of Homeopathy

On my first day of school, I learned that around 1825, homeopathy made its way to the United States, brought by several physicians from Europe. It became quite popular: By 1910, one out of four medical doctors in the U.S. were homeopaths, and homeopathy was taught in a number of medical schools and used in hospitals, doctors' offices, and by laypeople. In 1900, a monument was dedicated to Dr. Hahnemann, as the great medical reformer of the 19th century, by the American Institute of Homeopathy; President McKinley attended the dedication ceremony. This monument sits at Scott Circle, just one and a half miles from the White House.

So what happened? Why was homeopathic medicine removed from our health-care system? Sadly, competing market forces came into play: The Flexner Report of 1910 revolutionized the nature of medical education in the United States, establishing the biomedical model as the standard of training. The homeopathic community wasn't unified enough to withstand the political forces of the day, and by 1940 it was all but removed from our public medical institutions. Medical doctors who wished to practice homeopathy were told to stop or have their licenses revoked.

Nevertheless, homeopathy remained popular throughout the rest of the world, and among the elite and famous as well. There is a wonderful book entitled *The Homeopathic Revolution: Why Famous People and Cultural Heroes Choose Homeopathy* by Dana Ullman, M.P.H., which mentions movie stars, political figures, and spiritual teachers past and present who used homeopathy.

In the 200-year history of homeopathy, there were some very humorous stories as well. For example, when Dr. Hahnemann took up the task of creating this new system, there were many doctors who were against the idea of the law of similars; they wanted to prove Hahnemann wrong once and for all. The most honored doctors of the day would send their brightest students to study with Hahnemann undercover; surely these students would find that this new system did not work and expose him as a complete fraud. Quite the opposite occurred, however—these students saw the brilliance of homeopathy after practicing it themselves, and became some of the greatest practitioners of their time and staunch supporters of Hahnemann.

Homeopathy is making a comeback in the U.S., as people wish for a more natural system of medicine to restore their health and prevent disease.

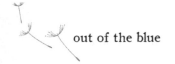

Miasms and Laws

For me, the most astonishing power of homeopathy rests in its ability to clear present traits *and* prevent inherited traits from being passed down by parents to their children, which Dr. Hahnemann referred to as "miasms." A miasm is a predisposition to certain diseases; modern science touches upon a form of this in the field of epigenetics. This includes the behaviors (mental/emotional states) our parents passed down, making us vulnerable to certain disease states, which are then passed down generation after generation unless they are mitigated or put in a dormant state with homeopathy.

Hahnemann researched chronic disease states and catalogued his findings, noticing that there were three major miasmatic (inherited) taints stemming from suppression of disease through the use of chemical drugs. A clear example of the law of suppression is in the case of eczema: When the condition is suppressed with cortisone, it can lead to asthma by moving the disharmony from the skin deeper into the system to the lungs; in Chinese medicine, it is known that the skin and lungs are connected. Suppressing itch from the skin, which is a major organ, and the body's attempt to rid itself of inner disharmony always creates a deeper internal disharmony in a more precious organ of the body, in this case the lungs.

The three major miasmatic taints (hereditary weaknesses) Hahnemann discovered are: (1) *Psoric miasm,* from suppressed scabies through the use of chemical drugs, expressed as complaints of anxiety, itch, weakness of organs, and low energy; (2) *Sycotic miasm,* from suppressed gonorrhea through the use of antibiotics, expressed as an overreaction on a cellular level such as cysts, tumors, overgrowth, and inflammatory conditions, and overreaction on a behavioral level such as high-energy, thrill-seeking activities; and (3) *Syphilitic miasm,* from suppressed syphilis through the use of chemical drugs expressed on the emotional level as hidden feelings, depression, addiction, alcoholism, and suicide, and on a physical level as destruction of structures such as physical deformities. There are two other mixed miasms—*Cancer* and *Tubercular*—which are combinations of the three primary ones. There is a wonderful book with case studies that describes all of this, called *The Foundation of the Chronic Miasms in the Practice of Homeopathy* by Henny Heudens-Mast.

I could easily understand my health issues by understanding the miasmatic states handed down to me by my ancestors. The good news is these energetic miasmatic states can be removed and/or lessened by the law of similars, with homeopathic care and a holistic approach to right living: good food, good work, good relationships, good exercise, good sleep, right thinking, and a spiritual understanding of our purpose on earth. Samuel Hahnemann was one of the first doctors to insist on a whole-life, mind/body/spirit approach to health.

Dr. Hahnemann's system of healing is simple yet profound, based on five fundamental principles: the law of similars; the single remedy; the minimal dose; serial dilutions (potentized remedy); and individualization, or treating the whole individual and not the disease. The proper direction of healing was also noted by Hahnemann and his renowned student Dr. Constantine Hering, known as the father of American homeopathy, by observing that you heal from the inside out, the top down, in reverse order of the appearance of symptoms.

Finally, all disease and behavioral states began to make sense to me once I understood the law of similars and the law of suppression; inherited miasmatic states; the powerful

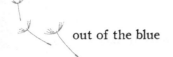

mind/body connection; and, most important, consciousness as the living, intelligent vital force that gives life to all the functions of the mind/body continuum and every cell of our being. It seems to me that the greatest crisis in our medical system is that of being blind to consciousness as the living force behind all externalized matter. Because of that, our understanding is limited to the physical world, mistaking the effect (symptoms) as the cause of disease rather than a reflection of a disharmony in our consciousness—living outside the body—that needs to be addressed.

I thought it ironic that the very symbol, the caduceus (see figure below), used to represent our medical system is an esoteric symbol of consciousness, mapping how our sacred consciousness innervates the physical body, thereby activating all life in our cells.

The symbol has two serpents wrapping around a central staff, which are the energy channels through which consciousness flows into the body on the breath. The two wings represent the third eye of spiritual knowing; and the spherical ball represents the crown chakra, where one experiences self-realization when all the forces of the two serpents and central staff flow upward, pass by the third eye, and settle in the crown chakra. If the time is right, the consciousness—now resting in the crown chakra—will remain in blissful unity, directing one's life force from that state. If not, it will flow down again, and although spiritually awake, one will still be under the influence of a dualistic state. (This is what had happened to me.) Since divine consciousness is the life force of the body, we must learn how to work with it to maintain our health and well-being.

By recognizing this divine consciousness as the primary source of all life, we can then move from a one-dimensional system of medicine that focuses only on the physical body to a multidimensional system that includes the mental, emotional, physical, and spiritual body acting as one unit. This principle of consciousness brings science and spirituality together, mending the split between the mind, body, and spirit as humanity concurrently mends this split.

It would only be a natural extension of our evolutionary growth as divine beings for our system of medicine to evolve in response. Then we would have the best trauma medicine and the best preventive and curative system that works in a gentle, affordable, and efficient way—inclusive of mind, body, *and* spirit.

When I made the choice to try homeopathy, I had no political ax to grind, nor was I married to any particular medical ideology; I just wanted to cure my condition without having to take pharmaceuticals for the rest of my life. Homeopathy worked to stop the progression of a weakened

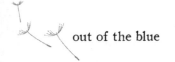

thyroid, as well as addressing the underlying cause, my mental/emotional state. Certainly my energy increased significantly, but I still needed the supplement, although at a lower dosage.

I know if I'd had homeopathic treatment much earlier in my life, instead of at age 55, I would have been able to totally return my thyroid to perfect working order. Chronic disease can cause damage to occur on the physical level, which may not be able to be restored completely using homeopathy; that's why it's so important to use it from a young age, to prevent damage and chronic health issues. I also would have understood the connection of grief and its effect on the thyroid, and paid even greater attention to clearing that grief.

It's Not about the Germs!

I wondered if homeopathy could cure my tendency toward getting a number of colds every winter—how would it deal with germs? I learned that Hahnemann stated germs don't *cause* disease; rather, a weakened vital force (our consciousness), which is affected by emotional and physical traumas, makes us *susceptible*. If we restore the vital force through the law of similars and health is restored, there's no need to kill the germs. I also read that on his deathbed, Louis Pasteur, the father of the germ theory of disease, recanted his original theory: He stated it isn't germs that cause disease, rather the inner terrain of the person makes them susceptible, just as Hahnemann had said.

I soon had many opportunities to put homeopathy's law of similars to the test regarding germs and the inner terrain. In the past, symptoms of my winter colds would start in my head and work their way down to my chest, sometimes causing bronchitis and the need for antibiotics.

After I studied homeopathy, and with the help of my practitioner, I began applying the law of similars and matched my cold symptoms, including my emotional/mental state, to the symptom picture of a remedy. I used *Arsenicum album* when a cold started in my head with a lot of sneezing and a clear runny nose, along with a feeling of restlessness and fatigue. If the symptoms progressed down to my chest, I used *Bryonia alba*—interestingly enough, this is also a remedy commonly needed for people who need Natrum muriaticum, my grief remedy. I learned that remedies have related affiliations with each other and affiliations with certain organs of the body.

In studying its history, I was equally astounded to learn that homeopathy had a long and effective history in all epidemics, including the 1918 flu pandemic. As Sandra J. Perko, Ph.D., C.C.N., chronicled in *The Homeopathic Treatment of Influenza,* millions of people died at that time, but those attended by medical doctors who only used homeopathic remedies lived. It was rare for any of these patients to die from the flu.

I tried certain remedies myself during the flu season, matching the remedy to current symptoms with immediate relief. Then I learned I could take the remedy as a preventive any time I heard that there were reports of the flu near me. Homeopathy doesn't necessarily worry about the strain of virus, as it does not treat disease but is concerned with matching the symptom picture.

Once I started using homeopathy to prevent and cure my colds and flu, I never needed to go back to antibiotics. More than that, homeopathy so strengthened my vital force that I rarely even get sick anymore. The remedies are

not aimed at killing germs; they simply restore harmony, and the symptoms disappear.

>

I was constantly astounded by homeopathy because I was taught that germs cause disease; it was complete heresy to think any other way! I could not deny that homeopathy worked in curing my colds . . . and it would soon be put to the test again in an incident involving my youngest daughter.

Deborah and her husband had come for a visit with my new grandson. They went out to dinner with friends, and a few hours later I heard a commotion at my front door. My daughter was calling for me, and she fell through the door writhing in pain. Her face was a mottled bluish-gray color. She looked like death!

"What's wrong?" I asked calmly, not wanting to show how distressed I felt at the sight of her. I even wondered if I should call an ambulance. She said she thought she had food poisoning and ran to the bathroom, bent over in extreme pain. Immediately, I remembered the remedy I had just learned for the symptom picture of acute food poisoning, Arsenicum album. I grabbed it from my kit, put two pellets in a small bottle of water—succussing it by hitting the bottom of the water bottle on the palm of my hand to make the energy of the remedy as strong as possible—and handed it to her through the slightly opened bathroom door.

I waited outside as she took a teaspoon of the remedy, thinking, *Will this really work? She's so sick.* I was half expecting to drive her to the emergency room, but after a few minutes, I heard my daughter say from the bathroom that she was feeling better now. "What? Better? What?!" I said in total amazement, as she walked out of the bathroom pain-free. Her face was a nice healthy pink color, far from the mottled bluish-gray I had just witnessed. I couldn't believe it—I *wouldn't* have believed it if I hadn't seen it with my own eyes! (Deborah learned later that her friend, who had eaten the same things at dinner, was sick for days with a terrible case of food poisoning.)

Over the years, incidents like this would happen again and again as I continued to study homeopathy and used it for my family, my friends, and myself. For instance, I once spent the night in a small beachfront motel. I noticed the bed sheets seemed a little musty, as did the mattress, but I figured it was only one night, what could go wrong? I soon came down with a horrible bout of scabies—from bed mites! I had never experienced anything like this before, and it really was awful. I was told by my regular medical doctor I would need to lather an antiparasite cream all over the affected areas of my skin, which would kill the nervous system of the mites. I wondered what it would do to me as well. Yet I was desperate with itching, so I got the cream and lathered it all over for days, feeling I was in a battle with those mites that lived under my skin. They just wouldn't die!

Then I remembered something—homeopathy. Surely if Hahnemann was right about matching the symptoms to the right remedy, harmony would be restored on the energetic level and the symptoms would abate. So I called my practitioner, who matched the symptoms to homeopathic Sulphur. I stopped the antiparasite cream, which wasn't working anyway, and took a dose of the remedy. Within a few minutes I felt the intensity of the itch abate. Each dose brought relief, and in a few days it was all gone—no mites, no itching, no more washing bed sheets and towels. Wow!

Sometime later, I got a call from a friend who had a terrible case of poison ivy all down her arm. She tried

various kinds of ointments with no results; her doctor put her on antibiotics for fear of infection, but that did not help, either. It was very red, spreading all over her arm, itching and oozing a sticky yellow liquid. Her symptom picture matched the homeopathic remedy picture of Graphites—she got the remedy and took the first dose, which immediately lessened the itching. There was continued improvement with each dose, and by the second day it was well on its way to resolving. By the third day it was completely healed: no redness, no itching, no oozing.

I had another friend whose cat scratched her face and it became very red and painful; nothing she did improved her symptoms. Her symptom picture matched the remedy *Ledum palustre*—she got the remedy, took a dose, and that's all she needed. Within minutes it became less painful, and a few hours later it was completely healed.

Yet another friend asked for advice after her own cat had bitten her on the arm. She was on a second round of antibiotics, but the arm was still red and painful and the tissue looked unhealthy. Her symptom picture also matched Ledum palustre—she already had a homeopathic kit at home and made up a remedy bottle, succussing it a few times before taking a dose. After the first dose of a capful, the arm felt less painful and was less red. After a second dose a number of hours later, it was even better and the tissue looked healthier. By the third dose the next day, the arm looked almost normal, with no redness and no pain. She took a fourth dose later that night, and her arm completely healed by morning.

There is a wonderful book chronicling the history of homeopathic medicine in the U.S. and the U.K., titled *The Faces of Homeopathy* by Julian Winston, which tells the story of homeopathic doctors in their own words. Over the years, the subject would continue to amaze me, leaving me shaking my head in disbelief, as well as delight!

Of course, as always, consult with a professionally trained practitioner to gain the knowledge and ability to include homeopathy in your health care.

serendipity

So many years passed . . . I had thought about writing down my spiritual experiences, but life kept getting busier. In the years that had gone by, Deborah had divorced her husband, and I'd moved in with her and my grandson, Nicolas, for three years. I'd been studying and sharing with friends about homeopathy, as well as practicing Reiki and massage. Life was good, and I finally felt positioned to increase my income. My grandson was now six years old and my daughter was about to get remarried, so I was moving into a new apartment.

I didn't fully appreciate how much self-generated stress I'd been under in the past few years. Being a type A personality and wired like a racehorse, I didn't realize the toll it was taking on me. I was about to find out.

It was a warm and sunny afternoon on July 30, 2006. I decided to take Nicolas to a nearby lake just four minutes from his house, and we had lunch on the beach and swam in the lake. At some point, I began to feel a pain in my upper back, which kept getting worse. Having always been a fairly healthy person, I started to become worried

and decided I'd better get help. I called my daughter, as I wanted her to come for my grandson, and told her that I thought I should go to the hospital. I had never said such a thing to her, so she knew something was very wrong. I hung up and dialed 911.

What I didn't know was that Deborah had immediately called her neighbor and our family friend, Ben, who was a paramedic. Then my daughter called 911 as well. Ben happened to be home for the first time in two weeks, and both he and Deborah rushed to the lake in separate cars. She got there first and saw a paramedic trying to set up some oxygen for me, and Ben arrived within moments. I was too sick to notice anyone.

On the way to the beach, Ben had called the paramedics and told them to be sure to take me to a particular hospital, where I would need to go for the proper medical care. He knew instinctively what I didn't know—that I was having a heart attack. I was later told by my cardiologist that if Ben hadn't been there, I would have been taken to a nearby hospital that did not have the special care I needed and would have died. But fate and destiny were on my side, and God's angels—in the form of doctors, paramedics, nurses, my daughter, and my grandson—were with me that day. I realized that if Nicolas had not been with me, I wouldn't have called my daughter first. If I hadn't called her first, then Ben wouldn't have been notified.

Within moments I was loaded into the ambulance with Ben by my side. As I lay on the gurney, he looked in my eyes and said, "Don't worry, Mary, I won't let you go." He said that with so much conviction, I felt completely safe and just let myself relax. At the same time I thought, *Go? Where would I go?* Another paramedic appeared, and after telling me that she would take good care of me, Ben went to the front of the ambulance to drive. The woman's face shone with grace and kindness; clearly, she loved her job. *She's God in action,* I thought.

There wasn't a moment to spare. I was so ill, but still didn't realize I was having a heart attack. Very quickly, I felt I was losing consciousness and closed my eyes. A familiar window of light appeared, and I instantly felt calm. I knew it was an entrance into heaven, and I felt the presence of God/Brahman. I no longer felt my body or heard any sounds, and I let myself completely rest in the light. Then I lost all consciousness.

When we arrived at the hospital, Ben opened the door of the ambulance to unload the gurney I was lying on, and I went into cardiac arrest. He instantly brought me back to life using cardiopulmonary resuscitation, and then I was whisked into the cardiac catheterization unit, where I received three stents. I was still unconscious and in critical condition.

After I was stabilized, I was taken to a larger hospital where I could have a bypass if needed. I was too ill for this, so instead received two more stents. Unfortunately, I suffered a femoral bleed from the procedure and the ambulance ride to the larger hospital, and I needed seven pints of blood along with vascular surgery to repair the hole in my femoral artery. My condition was so critical, I was given the last rites by a priest.

The doctors were amazed by my survival—and my poor family members, who had been through so much, were grateful to everyone who attended me with such grace, kindness, and skill.

❧

I had the heart attack on Sunday and was unconscious until Wednesday. I was in a drug-induced coma and had absolutely no awareness of anything—no light, no

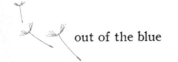

sound—yet I think I was in God's waiting room to see if I would stay or go. When I started to become conscious, I could hear the voice of Deborah, who was standing by my bedside. She was calling me back to this world by talking about things we had done together. She repeated a meditation mantra we often used, saying, "Remember?"

As I became conscious listening to her voice, I wanted to speak, but couldn't because of the breathing tube in my throat. In frustration, I tried to pull it out, but my hands were tied down. I gave up, falling back into the drug-induced coma. I drifted in and out of consciousness as they reduced the drugs; finally, the breathing tube was removed, but I have no memory of that moment.

When I awoke, I was stunned to find out all that had happened. I was told by the doctors that most people do not survive the kind of massive heart attack I had, which Ben called "the widow-maker." With a 2 percent survival rate, it was a miracle I was still alive. I'd had no previous symptoms of a heart attack, other than a sore feeling in my throat a few days beforehand. (Of course, there was a strong family history of heart problems, with my mother and her side of the family.) Many family members had also arrived, not only to see me, but for Deborah's wedding, which was to take place that Saturday. I truly felt that their loving presence had made all the difference in my ability to survive.

One of the first things I noticed when I started to become conscious was a lighter feeling in my heart. *What is this?* I wondered. I realized that by some divine intervention, a lot of old, unrecognized suffering I had felt in my heart beforehand was gone. This was incredible to me. *How could this happen?*

Although my heart felt so much lighter, physically I felt very weak. It took many days of resting in the hospital and a rehabilitation unit before I could regain any kind of energy to return home. That gave me a lot of time to think. As I reflected on my heart attack, although I felt some suffering had been released, I also realized that I still carried the habit of worrying about the future and for others close to me, as well as the sadness of too many losses in a life. I'd often think, *If only homeopathy had come into my life at a very early age, it could have been a life changer for me and my mother. Imagine if she had received treatment for her grief when she was forced to give up her baby as an unwed mother, and then when her own mother died while she was pregnant with me—perhaps I wouldn't have been born into so much grief from the very beginning of life.*

I also thought about how with homeopathy, in working with a practitioner, you gain an understanding of yourself and the reasons behind your symptoms so you can make the necessary emotional, mental, and physical adjustments in your life. On so many levels, my life stands as an example of why we need a system of medicine that deals with the whole person and their story on the level of mind/body/spirit, not just a physical level—we need an integrated system of medicine. The good news is that homeopathic medicine is here now, to be rejoined with trauma medicine to address the health of humanity on a whole new level, so we may be free in body, mind, and spirit to experience our health and divine nature in equal measure.

Finding My Calling

Since I couldn't go back to my usual work and needed many months of recuperation, I decided it must be time for me to share my story. My biggest focus now was writing,

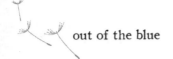

not only because it was the only thing I was physically able to do, but because I felt it was something I *had* to do; it felt like a calling. With that in mind, I wrote every day and at the end of nine months, self-published the first version of this book in 2007.

I then went back to work as a massage therapist and continued studying homeopathy, using it for myself, friends, and family. At some point, I realized so little was known in the U.S. about the practice that I had the idea of educating the public by offering small classes at my local natural market.

For the next five years, I taught the principles of homeopathy and some of the basic remedies to small groups of individuals, mainly mothers. The two-hour classes were taught in the early evening at a low cost. I would focus on applying the law of similars with regard to a particular topic like colds or the flu, or a list of common ailments like bee stings or poison ivy. Mothers loved being able to have an affordable, safe, natural approach for themselves and their families using over-the-counter remedies. I shared my hope that one day homeopathic medicine would be returned to our medical system, because we need all the tools possible to assist in caring for our health. I also volunteered my time at the market every Tuesday for an hour, answering questions about homeopathy.

Whenever I traveled around town, I'd often be approached by my former students, who shared their homeopathic success stories. One woman told me that she'd passed on what she learned about preventing colds and flu with her colleagues at work, and not one of them was out sick that winter, which had not been the case in the past. Another shared how when her daughter came down with symptoms of the flu, she matched the symptom picture to one of the remedies. To her amazement, her daughter became well overnight, and was able to attend school perfectly healthy the next day.

A Serendipitous Concussion Story

Fast-forward to January 2014, and I found myself walking into a conference room in Maui, Hawaii. As I wrote in the Author's Note at the beginning of this book, Dr. Wayne Dyer had invited me to attend his Divine Love weekend seminar as a surprise guest speaker.

All of the speakers had been invited to meet each other here in the conference room, and find out the agenda for the weekend. That's when I was first introduced to Scarlett Lewis, author of *Nurturing Healing Love*. As we all chatted together, Scarlett mentioned that she had a concussion and was not feeling well. She wondered how she was going to give her hour-long talk the next day.

What follows is a wonderful story of synchronistic events. I'll let Scarlett tell the story in her own words:

> Roughly a year following the shooting death of my six-year-old son, Jesse, at Sandy Hook Elementary School, I was walking on a sidewalk backward, saying good-bye to my stepson and urging him to be careful driving, when I tripped on a crack, smashing my head into the pavement. Dazed and confused, I had to be helped up and into my stepson's house by his mother, where I stumbled onto the couch to rest. I remained prone with ice on my bleeding head for over an hour. Even though I didn't feel well, I needed to drive my son and myself home.
>
> On the way home, I happened to pass by a hospital and felt I really should get checked out, as I thought I might have a concussion. It turns out I was right. The doctors said it was a fairly bad one and sent me home, advising me to take painkillers. I took Excedrin every four

hours for the pain, which did not help at all. Along with my concussion, I had a huge lump on my head where it was scraped and had been bleeding. The doctors had told me it would take a while for the symptoms to go away but hadn't given me a time frame of when they would resolve.

I was leaving to speak at a Wayne Dyer conference in Maui two days later. When I arrived, I was having terrible debilitating headaches and was afraid they might affect my ability to give a clear, coherent talk in front of over 600 people the following two days. In the conference room before the seminar, I met Mary Ter-hune, who was introduced as another author as well as a homeopathic educator and nurse. I asked if she had a natural remedy for concussion, and she said she always travels with her over-the-counter remedies for herself. Before she left to the conference, she'd felt an urge to pack the one for symptoms of concussion—she literally said that she'd heard a message to pack the remedy as someone at the conference might need it! She said homeopathy doesn't diagnose or treat diseases or symptoms; rather, it matches the symptom picture of the person to a remedy that matches those symptoms, and through the law of similars, harmony is restored and symptoms abate on their own. After the miraculous journey following Jesse's death, I believed this was another divinely inspired moment of serendipity. I figured the remedy might work, and since it was over the counter with no side effects, why not try it.

Following the group meeting, a few of us went with Mary back to her hotel room to get her remedy kit. I took one of the tiny white pellets of the homeopathic remedy *Natrum sulphuricum* from her kit, and put it in a small bottle of water. Mary showed me how to succuss the bottle to make a dose stronger each time, by striking the bottom of the bottle on my palm two times. When

I got back to my room, I took my first dose of one capful from the water bottle. Mary had said I might only need one dose, since the potency of the remedy was powerful enough to match the strong symptoms I was experiencing. If there were no more symptoms the next day, I need not repeat the remedy, since the remedy is only given if the symptom picture remains present. We would see.

Mary had told me that I might have a remedy dream to let me know that it's working, or I might not. Sleep came easily that night, perhaps for the first time since Jesse's murder. Upon closing my eyes and falling asleep, I began to see little drops of blood in my head that multiplied and swirled, and then my sight became fully red. I had visions of flying and being totally free. When I awoke the next morning, I felt refreshed, with no head pain. I was astonished—my head felt 99 percent clear, the swelling was gone, and the scrape on my head disappeared overnight. Hard to believe, but true.

I called Mary to report success! We discussed that I might take one more dose so that I would feel absolutely 100 percent. I did, after succussing the bottle twice, and felt completely healed and back to normal within hours. Mary had also mentioned a remedy commonly known to athletes and mothers, *Arnica montana*, as its remedy picture includes bumps and bruises because it's a good blood absorber, so I took a dose of that as well. I was able to give my hour talk with ease and without any pain or discomfort whatsoever, and none of the symptoms ever returned!

I vowed to remain in contact with Mary and share the great news of this natural curative system as a safe and effective choice for parents to use for themselves and their families in common acute events. I also want to see this natural medicine returned to our health-care system so that all doctors and nurses can add it to their

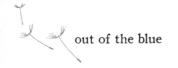

emergency medicine bags and educate the public about this system.

I'd like to report another follow-up. Since the night Jesse died, I had trouble sleeping and took sleeping pills. I'd continued to take them until I met Mary and took the remedy. For some reason, my sleep began to get better, even though I know Mary didn't give me anything for it. It seemed that the remedy returned my state to one of inner harmony, and a normalized sleep naturally followed and continues. Many months later, I shared with Mary how my sleep improved, and she informed me that a big part of the remedy picture of Natrum sulphuricum, apart from head trauma, is also *grief!* How remarkable that I would come to take this particular remedy.

The story of Mary being invited by Dr. Dyer to the seminar was miraculous enough, but then Mary being urged inwardly to bring this particular remedy was extraordinary. And our meeting that Friday evening in the conference room was absolute divine serendipity!

Scarlett and I remain in contact with each other today, with the purpose in mind of sharing the sweet wisdom of this natural system to support others in their healing. I remain always in awe of this system of medicine that continues to be affordable and without side effects in service to humanity.

The Paradigm Shifts We Need to Make

The amazing results from homeopathy make me envision a day when there will be homeopathic educational groups in every town, staffed by homeopathic nurses, and moms who will teach others to care for themselves and their families by using their own remedy kits at home.

The old motto of teaching a person how to fish is still the best way to empower others, and it's a most efficient and sustainable approach to health care.

I believe that being in charge of one's own health is an essential part of becoming a master of one's life, and I know for certain it is possible given the response of the small group of individuals and moms at my local natural market. I focus a lot on health because good health frees us to have the energy to focus our minds to turn inward, release our emotional blocks, and connect with our divine spiritual energy.

Below is a list of emerging paradigm shifts I foresee for humanity:

- Consciousness lives *outside* the body, existing beyond time and space. It does not come *from* the body/brain; rather, it innervates and informs the body/brain. It is the omniscient operating system of the body/mind/spirit and universe, divine in both origin and nature. This knowledge will completely change our medical system.

- Since we are beings of consciousness, we need consciousness-based systems of medicine to assist in maintaining harmony in our body/mind/spirit continuum releasing disease states. I see homeopathy and acupuncture, both of which are these types of systems, playing major roles in the evolution of the consciousness of humanity.

- Prevention-based medicine will no longer use material chemicals to stimulate the immune system; rather, high-dilution, affordable remedies will prove the healing power of

the vital force (our consciousness), both in prevention and cure, without side effects and according to nature's innate law of similars and healing.

- Nurses and homeopaths will teach this consciousness-based medicine to the public, creating healers in every household and freeing emergency-room doctors and nurses for trauma-based medicine. The two systems of homeopathy and allopathy will become unified, bringing a more balanced approach to our health and well-being.

- The consciousness-based medicine of homeopathy will be returned to our medical system. People will regain the power to heal themselves through education in this system, and diseases will diminish significantly, even those thought to be incurable. This is already beginning to happen—see the first Homeopathy Academy for Moms (www.homeopathycenter .org/homeopathy-academy-moms).

- We are awakening from the suffering dream and story of the ego/mind-centered consciousness to the bliss of divine-centered consciousness, our true self.

- Self-realization is our natural state and birthright, not the ego/mind story. We are remembering our true nature; we are God/ Brahman, here to bring heaven on earth.

- The ego is a temporary construct of iden-tification that disappears as we become in perfect union with our divine nature; it is not needed to survive.

These paradigms are already here, waiting in the wings for us to awaken to them. By reclaiming our divine identity, we will be able to move past the old paradigms of disease-based medicine and ego-driven minds toward new solutions in all areas of endeavor.

afterword

It is now the spring of 2015, and I continue to work as a therapeutic massage therapist, helping to educate my clients in caring for themselves and encouraging them to become knowledgeable stewards of their health and spiritual well-being. Everyone is feeling the need for new approaches to a more fulfilling spiritual inner life and new ways to become healthier, wishing for natural ways to achieve and maintain wellness. Everyone feels the stresses and strains of a world in disorder and the need to bring greater balance to our lives.

The world stands on the precipice of a huge spiritual transition, one that has never before been possible en masse. We are realizing that we can no longer survive using the ego-based mind to drive our lives or our planet. Our ego is behind the continued feeling of separation from each other, and fuels our unexamined and unreleased sorrows through feelings of shaming and blaming ourselves.

We can take simple but powerful steps right now to engage our divine nature and keep connected with it in every moment. For example, we need to heal with others—we must find compassionate friends, healers, and groups

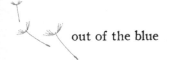

who understand the process of releasing emotional pain and the goal of reclaiming our divine nature. We're all in this together.

Here are a few suggestions for those just beginning the journey or for those who have been on the journey for a long time. These are the things I do:

1. Create positive changes in life by making a vision board. Buy a piece of 20" x 30" poster board and put statements and pictures on it that remind you of what you want in your life. Place on it what you want to see right now: it could be about optimal physical or financial health, family happiness, good relationships, spiritual understandings, embracing forgiveness, love, supportive friends, a warm and inviting home, or just remembering to breathe! Anything that supports and nurtures you while keeping the goal in mind of reclaiming your divine nature; anything inwardly or outwardly that supports that goal is what to keep in the
forefront. Put the board in a place where you can easily see it every day.

2. Take moments throughout the day to consciously connect with your breathing. Just watching it go in and out immediately connects you in this very moment with your divine nature, the giver of this life force that rides on your breath.

3. Go out in nature. Even just stepping outside to notice a tree or flower, the sky, the clouds, or the wind—all this connects you to divinity, and the peace and healing that naturally abides in nature.

4. When you go for a walk, connect with your breath and give thanks to Mother Nature for her beauty, company, and healing balms. If you like, you can also choose to inwardly repeat a mantra that reminds you of your divine nature, like *Om,* or *I am that I am,* or even *Thank you.*

5. Clean out your closets of stuff. Recycle it, give it away, sell it—whatever way you do it, clear it out. It frees up energy and makes way for new things, both tangible and intangible.

6. Gently allow yourself room to feel your feelings. Allow yourself time to cry when you feel like it. Sometimes it feels right to cry alone with the divine as your witness, and sometimes it helps to call an understanding friend or see a compassionate healer—just don't stuff your feelings. Feeling and releasing makes space to connect with the divine within. We become fully human in this process of becoming fully divine.

7. Avail yourself of the wonderful healing modalities of homeopathy, acupuncture, massage, chiropractic, meditation, and yoga, which support transformation and health and harmonize the body/mind/spirit continuum.

8. Whatever you do, keep going, even if you can only take baby steps. Don't let anything deter you from reclaiming your true divine nature. It's yours; it belongs to you. I know this for certain, and I am here with you—we are traveling together. Extraordinary things can happen when we

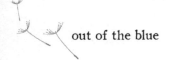

embrace our divine path: a new life emerges,
a new earth is born.

The direct message from God/Brahman still rings in
my ears, and it's a message I hope to share in seminars
and with groups as I travel around the world when this
book is published:

> *Here is your divinity,*
> *the divinity that awaits all mankind.*
> *Your soul wants full expression now.*
> *This is the presence.*
> *This is the living presence.*
> *This is living. This is real.*

May grace always be with us.

acknowledgments

First and foremost, I want to thank my spiritual teacher, who for the last 29 years has guided me and continues to guide me to self-realization. Such teachers are rare, and it has been my great fortune to be in the company of one who has made the journey.

I also want to thank all the saints and great ones from all religions and all spiritual paths who are shining examples of the light of God within, beckoning us to take the inner adventure to discover the same truth within: God/ Brahman.

On this earthly journey, I want to especially thank my daughters, who inspire me and make me so proud of the wonderful people and mothers they have become. Thanks and love to my grandchildren, who are full of life and make me laugh; they are such a blessing to this world.

Thanks go to all of those wonderful friends in my life who have supported me in body and soul in various roles along the way, especially my friend and colleague Susan M. Duffy, who shared in my journey to bring this book to a larger audience while offering helpful

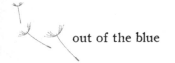

insights. Thanks also to Farah Gron for her helpful editorial contributions and comments. Thanks as well to Richard and Karima Spencer for their beautiful friendship and support, always valuing the message of this book. Thanks to Scarlett Lewis for generously sharing her incredible experience with consciousness-based medicine.

To Dr. Wayne Dyer, a very special thank-you, and many more to come, for that fortuitous midnight call! It isn't often we meet someone whose generosity can change our life in the most amazing ways, opening doors once closed. Thanks also to Raymond Moody, M.D., Ph.D., for his continued friendship and pioneering work in the field of near-death experiences (NDEs), and for our inspiring conversations as we met over numerous breakfasts and dinners at an NDE seminar where he was a headline speaker, as well as very recently at a seminar in California.

A very special thanks to my acupuncturist, friend, and colleague, Ann McKinney, for showing up in my life at just the right time, profoundly deepening the healing of the wounds in my life through the power of this magnificent ancient healing modality.

My heartfelt thanks to all my friends at the meditation center who have offered their prayers and support in every way for my benefit during my health challenge. One can never know the reach of those prayers, and I am filled with gratitude for your kind offerings.

A special thanks is offered to those who saved my life on the day of my near-fatal heart attack. Miracles happen, and on that fateful day in July 2006, a miracle happened to me. To Ben Podsiadlo, my neighbor and family friend, who was my paramedic that day and performed cardiopulmonary resuscitation that kept me alive, I give my unending gratitude and love. Our two families became one that day. He also skillfully organized all the personnel who had an active role in saving my life—to all the paramedics, doctors, nurses, and hospital staff, thank you for your dedication and skill, delivered with so much care and love. May God bless you in your service to humanity.

Appreciation goes to all the teachers in my life who have enlightened me along the way with their knowledge in the fields of medicine; nursing; bodywork; Reiki; and, in particular, homeopathy, the crown jewel of my healing journey. A special thank you to my friend and homeopathic teacher, Luc De Schepper, M.D., for initiating me into the miraculous science and study of homeopathic medicine; there are not enough words to describe my gratitude. Through witnessing Dr. Luc's compassion, intelligence, and skill in case-taking, I became a better practitioner and a better person, as he showed me the essence of true healing.

Homeopathy deserves a special mention because it has so profoundly transformed my understanding of the origin of disease on the emotional, psychological, and physical level and the nature of true healing. It is simply the most elegant and efficacious system of consciousness-based medicine awaiting mankind to cure our ills, prevent disease, and restore our health—from simple colds to chronic diseases to afflicted hearts and minds. May it be restored to our health-care system, standing as an equal partner next to our extraordinary and esteemed system of trauma-based medicine in service to humanity.

ABOUT THE AUTHOR

Joanne Shapiro, www.joanneshapiro.com

Mary Terhune has been in the healing arts for over 40 years, journeying as a registered nurse from allopathy to the consciousness-based medicine of homeopathy, body-centred therapeutic massage and Reiki. After practising Western medicine for over 15 years in various settings including hospitals, nursing homes and a medical office, Mary discovered natural medicine out of the need to heal herself and her family. She studied at Holy Name Hospital in New Jersey, as well as the Cambridge Institute for Muscular Therapy and the Renaissance Institute of Classical Homeopathy, both in the Boston area.

Mary also has a degree in sociology from Boston College. For 16 years, she served as an administrative assistant, managing the office and organizing international conferences for the Center for Theoretical Geo/Cosmo Plasma Physics at the Massachusetts Institute of Technology.

Mary currently lives and works in a quiet rural town in New England near her family; she has two daughters, five grandchildren and two great-grandchildren. She practises meditation and has been studying Eastern philosophy, has travelled to India and has a self-realized meditation master as her guide to the inner knowledge and experience of self-realization.

www.maryterhune.com

notes

notes

notes

notes

notes

notes

HAY HOUSE

Look within

Join the conversation about latest products,
events, exclusive offers and more.

 Hay House UK

 @HayHouseUK

 @hayhouseuk

 healyourlife.com

We'd love to hear from you!